APOCRYPHA FOR BEGINNERS

APOCRYPHA
FOR BEGINNERS

A Guide to Understanding
and Exploring Scriptures
Beyond the Bible

BRANDON W. HAWK

ROCKRIDGE
PRESS

Interior and Cover Designer: Jane Archer
Art Producer: Janice Ackerman
Editors: Lauren O'Neal and Adrian Potts
Production Editor: Jenna Dutton
Production Manager: Holly Haydash

Author photo courtesy of Susan J. Hawk.
Illustration courtesy of iStock and Shutterstock.

ISBN: Print 978-1-64876-627-5
        eBook 978-1-64876-129-4
R0

For all of my students—past,
present, and future.

CONTENTS

INTRODUCTION

Welcome to a beginner's guide to the wide world of literature known as biblical apocrypha. Broadly defined, apocrypha are works that deal with biblical subjects or that are attributed to biblical figures even though they did not make it into the Bible. There are countless apocrypha to discover. In this book, I discuss more than fifty of these apocrypha, including some of the most important for the histories of Judaism and Christianity, as well as some of my personal favorites. I have not included the texts of apocrypha themselves—which could fill many volumes, each the size of the Bible itself!—but I provide explanations of each work, where it came from, what it says, and why it is interesting or important. My hope is that by reading these introductions, you will be inspired to explore apocrypha more deeply.

If you do wish to read any of the apocryphal texts discussed in this book, you can find many in translations online and in print. See Further Reading (page 136) for resources on where they can be found.

Much of my own teaching and research revolves around these apocrypha. While earning my MA and PhD in medieval studies, I fell in love with this subject, and over the years I have continued to explore apocrypha. In particular, my own research and publications have focused on how apocrypha circulated, how they were received in the medieval period, and what all of this tells us about the diversity of religious beliefs across the history of Christianity.

I have introduced students to these apocrypha and find that they offer both entertainment and new ways of seeing the world. I hope that you will find the same thing, as these apocrypha provide snapshots of what different people have imagined as they sought to understand their own relationships with the divine.

CHAPTER ONE

What Are Apocrypha?

When we think about the Bible, most of us, religious or not, think of it as a specific book with a set table of contents, or the "gospel truth" for Christians. But the Bible hasn't always existed in its current form. In fact, the Bible does not exist in just one form right now, since biblical content varies among different faith communities. How was the Bible put together? Who decided what individual books belonged in it? Were certain books lost, censored, or left out of the Bible? If so, what happened to them? This chapter will tell the origin story of the scriptures that made it into the Bible and those that did not—otherwise known as apocrypha.

The Genesis of the Bible

Before we can talk about what is not in the Bible, we need to understand how the Bible itself came to be. Although the concept of "the Bible" differs across faith traditions, there is core content that largely overlaps in different traditions. Content in the Bible is called the "canon"—scriptures, or holy texts. The word "canon" comes from the Greek *kanon*, meaning "rule" or "measuring stick," and took on a specialized sense to signify an authoritative collection of works. Below we will look more closely at what is included in the biblical canon.

THE HEBREW BIBLE

The core of the biblical canon is made up of the Hebrew Bible, or what Christians call the "Old Testament." It includes a collection of literature—myths, histories, parables, songs, prophecies, laws, and more—written over hundreds of years by dozens of authors, each with a different reason for writing. In Hebrew, this collection is called the Tanakh, a name derived from an acronym for its three main parts: Torah (Law), Nevi'im (Prophets), and Ketuvim (Writings).

The precise details of the canonization of the Hebrew Bible are difficult to determine, but the process occurred over several hundred years after the Persian king Cyrus the Great allowed the Jews to return to Palestine from exile in Babylon (539 BCE), and until sometime in the decades after the destruction of the Second Temple in 70 CE. Basic ideas about the canon of the Hebrew Bible began to solidify during the Second Temple period—the time between 516 BCE, when the original temple in Jerusalem was rebuilt after being destroyed by the Babylonians, and 70 CE, when it was destroyed again by the Romans (never to be rebuilt).

The Hebrew Bible has survived in a few major forms, most notably the Masoretic Text (MT) and the Septuagint (LXX). Both of these have been the basis for major translations of the Bible into many other languages.

THE MASORETIC TEXT

The Masoretic Text, written in Hebrew, was produced in early medieval Palestine and is considered the canonical Bible in Judaism today. This form of the Hebrew Bible was standardized within Rabbinic Judaism (ca. 70–600 CE), which focused on intensive interpretation of the Torah by the rabbis and developed as the mainstream form of Judaism by the sixth century. The Hebrew Bible as it was passed down during this time was based on earlier "witnesses" (copies of handwritten manuscripts) and eventually became solidified as the standard form. This standardization occurred primarily as a result of the efforts of a group of Jews called the Masoretes, who copied, edited, and distributed the handwritten manuscripts of the Hebrew Bible between the seventh and tenth centuries. The books that the Masoretic Text comprises are known as the "protocanon"—books that are canonical in not only Judaism but also every denomination of Christianity.

THE SEPTUAGINT

The Septuagint is a collection of Greek translations of the books of the Hebrew Bible produced between the third and second centuries BCE by Greek-speaking Jews living in Alexandria, Egypt. The first translation was of the Torah, followed by translations of the rest of the Tanakh and other deuterocanonical works (more on this next and in chapter 2). A legend developed that the Greek text of the Torah was created by seventy scholars working independently, who all came up with the same translation—which gave rise to the term

"Septuagint" (or LXX, for seventy). Eventually, Greek versions of the whole Hebrew Bible were collected and came to be known as the Septuagint. Some of the most important witnesses include the Greek Bibles (with both Old and New Testaments) known as the Codex Vaticanus (created ca. 300–325 CE), Codex Sinaiticus (ca. 330–360 CE), and Codex Alexandrinus (ca. 400–440 CE).

THE CHRISTIAN BIBLE

As Christianity developed, so did ideas and questions about what works Christians should accept as authoritative. Should the Hebrew scriptures be accepted? What other works by founding figures of Christianity should be read as scriptures? The contents of what eventually became the New Testament took a few centuries to solidify. This section provides an overview of the formation of the Christian Bible as a canon. (See Appendix A on page 129 for a full timeline and Appendix B on page 132 for a full comparison of different canons.)

THE EARLIEST CANONS

In the first few centuries after the life of Jesus, there was no established form of orthodoxy (accepted doctrine of belief), and the beliefs and practices of Christianity were hotly debated—including the biblical canon. At times, different authorities leveled claims of heresy (incorrect beliefs and practices) at those they disagreed with, or at works of scripture they considered to be outside their preferred canon.

The best evidence for what early Christians considered to be canonical appears in lists of works held to be authoritative. Different early Christians had their own lists, and the contents varied depending on the theological stance of the authors. Notable early lists are those by the theologians Origen, Eusebius, and Athanasius. In fact, Athanasius's list in his *39th Festal Letter* (composed in 367 CE) includes the twenty-seven books of the New Testament most familiar today and is often hailed as the definitive statement on the Christian canon. Some early Christians drew up lists of apocrypha to contrast with the canon, as in the *Pseudo-Gelasian Decree* (composed ca. 519 and 553 CE), which catalogs apocryphal works that it says Christians should reject.

THE COUNCIL OF ROME

By the middle of the fourth century, consensus had largely formed around ideas like orthodoxy, theological concepts, and the contents of the accepted canon. In 382, Pope Damasus I convened a meeting of different bishops from across the Roman Empire to affirm the canon of the Christian Bible. This event is now known as the Council of Rome and is often considered a watershed for the establishment of the biblical canon—at least, for the Western Catholic Church. At this time, Pope Damasus charged Jerome, a scholar and priest, with translating the Hebrew Bible and Greek New Testament into Latin. Jerome worked on this project between 382 and 405, and it later became known as "the Vulgate," which was the standard form of the Bible known across Western Europe throughout the medieval period.

THE CHALCEDONIAN AND GREAT SCHISMS

Many of the theological debates of early Christianity came to a head at different ecumenical councils of church leaders. The Council of Chalcedon was particularly significant because it resulted in the schism of the Oriental Orthodox Churches; in other words, the Oriental Orthodox leaders separated from the rest of Christianity represented at the council. Eventually, major theological differences emerged among other Christian communities. Differences between Roman Catholic and Eastern Orthodox leaders reached a climax in 1054, resulting in the East–West Schism (also known as the Great Schism). While these schisms did not happen because of divergent views of the biblical canon, the differences across these communities are substantial.

THE PROTESTANT REFORMATION

Another major split occurred in the sixteenth century, with the Protestant Reformation. As Protestants distanced themselves from Roman Catholicism, they rejected certain books of the Roman Catholic form of the Bible that they categorized as the "deutero-canonical" works. These were all early Jewish works included in the Latin Vulgate (and that still are part of the Roman Catholic Bible). Protestants began to separate them out, sometimes printing them in Bibles under the title *The Apocrypha* and eventually leaving them out altogether.

NOTABLE VERSIONS OF THE BIBLE

The Bible has been transmitted across the history of Judaism and Christianity in several important forms. These are listed in chronological order of origin.

MASORETIC TEXT: Authoritative text of the Hebrew Bible, standardized ca. 600–1000 CE (even though texts circulated much earlier).

SEPTUAGINT: Greek translation of the Hebrew Bible, ca. 250–50 BCE.

VULGATE: Latin translation of the Hebrew Bible and Greek New Testament undertaken by Jerome, 382–405 CE.

DOUAY-RHEIMS: English translation of the Latin Vulgate undertaken by Catholic translators, published 1582–1610.

AUTHORIZED/KING JAMES VERSION: English translation of the Hebrew Bible and Greek New Testament undertaken by English Protestant translators, published in 1611.

FLUID SCRIPTURES

As already noted, certain scriptures are apocryphal to some Jews and Christians but canonical (or deuterocanonical) to others. For instance, some deuterocanonical books are accepted by Beta Israel Jews as well as Roman Catholic, Eastern Orthodox, Oriental Orthodox, and Assyrian Church of the East Christians, even though they are not accepted by Protestants and were never part of the standard Masoretic Hebrew Bible (this will be discussed in chapter 2). Eastern Orthodox and Orthodox Tewahedo Christians have different biblical canons, and some of their scriptures are considered apocryphal by Western Christians. This book will highlight differences in accepted forms of the Bible among Judaism, Roman Catholicism, Eastern Orthodoxy, and Ethiopian Orthodoxy, with some references to other communities as appropriate.

CANON, APOCRYPHA, OR SOMETHING ELSE?

The works considered canonical or apocryphal differ among religious faiths. Even within those broad categories, there are further distinctions still. This list provides a handy glossary of the key terms used to describe the authority of works within certain communities.

ANTILEGOMENA: Works of disputed or doubted authenticity and authority as scripture; from the Greek word meaning "spoken against."

APOCRYPHA: Works about biblical subjects or attributed to biblical figures that were not included in the canonical Bible; from the Greek word meaning "hidden."

CANONICAL: Works accepted as authoritative scriptures; from the Greek word meaning "rule" or "measuring stick."

DEUTEROCANON: Works accepted as part of the Old Testament by the Roman Catholic, Eastern Orthodox, Oriental Orthodox, and Assyrian Church of the East Christians, even though they are not accepted by Protestants and were never part of the Hebrew Bible; from the Greek word meaning "second canon."

PROTOCANON: Works in the Hebrew Bible accepted by all Jewish and Christian communities as canonical.

PSEUDEPIGRAPHA: Works attributed to a certain figure as the author, even though the work was not written by that person; from the Greek word meaning "falsely ascribed."

Noncanonical Scriptures

Some Jewish and Christian works are not considered canonical by anyone: They have never been included in any formal definition of the canonical Bible. This type of literature makes up the largest group of apocrypha. Some of these apocrypha were written at the same time as works included in the Bible, others were written in response to books of the Bible, and still others were written to address questions not answered in the Bible. Many of these apocrypha have been considered authoritative and important in their own right, even though they have never been formally recognized the same way canonical scriptures have been.

The reasons why these apocrypha were never canonized are myriad and complex. In some cases, they contradict canonical scriptures or voices who were seen as the most authoritative (or loudest) in early Christianity. But in many other cases, they accord quite well with the canonical Bible. Some of the reasons are due to personal preferences on the part of early Christian authorities. Quite a few apocrypha were composed after the biblical canon had been settled. While certain apocrypha were censored at different times, many became popular and some were given a status of authority; several were even included in the same pages as the canonical works. The history of each apocryphal work reveals a unique case for exploring these issues.

This book will cover a wide variety of noncanonical works, from early Jewish compositions like those included among the Dead Sea Scrolls (see chapter 4) to Christian apocrypha. As you will see, there are a multitude of varieties to explore.

The Hebrew Bible was composed mainly in Hebrew (with some Aramaic in Daniel and Ezra), and the New Testament was composed in Greek, but these have been translated into many languages across the history of Judaism and Christianity. Apocrypha were composed in and translated into many of the same languages.

The following list describes the most common languages you will see referred to throughout this book. It is worth noting that in the late antique and medieval periods, apocrypha were translated into many other languages besides those listed here—across Afro-Eurasia, including Western Europe, North and East Africa, the Middle East, China, and India.

ARABIC: This language emerged in pre-Islamic Arabia and became the lingua franca of the Middle East with the spread of Islam. It has been a common language for many Christians and Muslims, and it is the language of Islam's sacred text, the Qur'an.

ARAMAIC: One of the common languages of the Near East during the Second Temple and medieval periods, related to Hebrew. Jesus most likely spoke a form of Aramaic.

ARMENIAN: Historically spoken in the Armenian Highlands, it is now the official language of Armenia.

COPTIC: The latest stage of the Egyptian language, based on the older form once written in hieroglyphs. It was first used in the second century CE.

GE'EZ: The Classical Ethiopic language spoken in ancient and medieval Ethiopia and Eritrea, still used in the liturgy of the Orthodox Tewahedo Church.

GREEK: The lingua franca of the Hellenistic world around the Mediterranean and in the Near East in antiquity. This language was used by many across Afro-Eurasia, including pagans, Jews, and Christians, in antiquity and through the Middle Ages.

HEBREW: This language was spoken by the inhabitants of Israel in antiquity and up to about 400 CE. Many works of the Bible and apocrypha were composed in Hebrew; it is still used in Jewish worship, and some communities still speak it regularly.

LATIN: The language of the Roman Empire, it was used by many across Afro-Eurasia, including pagans, Jews, and Christians, from antiquity through the Middle Ages.

CHURCH SLAVIC: A Slavic language that was standardized in the ninth century, it was used for Christian literature throughout the medieval period.

SYRIAC: This language derives from Aramaic and was used across the Near East, especially Mesopotamia, between the first and fifteenth centuries. It is a major language for many Eastern Christian communities.

What Can We Learn from Apocrypha?

Sometimes people want to learn from apocrypha about Jesus or the biblical world. But apocrypha do not convey actual first-hand accounts as much as they tell us what different Jews and Christians have believed about biblical subjects for various theological reasons.

Often when apocrypha are featured in the media, they are framed by sensationalized accounts that gain a lot of attention. But this is mainly because it can be easy for us not to look beyond assumptions based on our own traditions or religious foundations. One prominent example is the *Gospel of Mary* (page 88): While many have jumped to conclusions about this work as evidence for Jesus's marital relationship with Mary Magdalene—leading to controversy among practicing Christians—scholars remain interested in it more for what it reveals about early Christian beliefs.

Many apocrypha provide a look beyond our own culture and assumptions. This can be especially illuminating for those who grew up in Western Christian communities. After all, there is much to learn from apocrypha held sacred by others.

INSIGHT INTO HISTORY

Many apocrypha provide contexts for the Bible as well as the history of Judaism and Christianity. For instance, *1–2 Maccabees* (pages 23 and 25) provide historical accounts of Palestine during the Second Temple period. The Dead Sea Scrolls provide knowledge about Judaism as it was practiced during Jesus's life. The authors of the New Testament read and took ideas from certain Jewish apocrypha, like the author of the canonical Epistle of Jude using a quotation from *1 Enoch* (page 114). Similarly, early Jewish apocalyptic writings help us understand some of Jesus's teachings in the canonical Gospels and the enigmatic book of Revelation.

Apocrypha can also illuminate history in other ways. From works composed in different places, at different times, and from different perspectives, we can gain significant insights into the rise and fall of civilizations, the lives and practices of those who lived in them, and how diverse belief systems have formed and flourished throughout the ages.

THE SURPRISING LEGACY OF APOCRYPHA

Even Christians who reject apocrypha might embrace their ideas without knowing it. For example, the "ox and ass" referred to in the Christmas carol "What Child Is This?" come from the *Gospel of Pseudo-Matthew*. Although the Apostles' Creed (recited by millions of Roman Catholics, Protestants, and other Christians) includes a phrase about Christ descending into hell, popular imagery about his journey to the underworld comes from the *Gospel of Nicodemus*. The *Apocalypse of Paul* was so significant in Western Europe during the Middle Ages that it influenced doctrines about the afterlife that continue to inform Roman Catholic and Protestant theologies. Plenty of other examples exist, too.

RELIGIOUS DIVERSITY

Probably the most important thing we can learn about from apocrypha is diversity. Although these works were only sometimes included in certain biblical collections, they speak to a plurality of beliefs and practices in the history of Judaism and Christianity. In fact, the inclusion of some apocrypha in different biblical canons demonstrates this even more fully. Yet even certain apocrypha that were never included in any biblical canons were widespread and popular over the centuries. After all, Jews and Christians do not follow some monolithic approach to religion, but adhere to many different beliefs and practices.

It might be best to think about these apocrypha as representatives of dynamic "Judaisms" and "Christianities" rather than any single, static religion.

Because of such diversity, apocrypha provide perspectives on Christianity that would otherwise be lost. For example, many apocrypha feature women in prominent roles. One well-known example is Judith (page 18), but the stories of Susanna and the Elders (page 30), *Joseph and Aseneth* (page 38), and the *Acts of Paul and Thecla* (page 97) center on women, too. Elsewhere, the *Infancy Gospel of James* (page 65) and the *Gospel of Pseudo-Matthew* (page 67) put the Virgin Mary on center stage; and gnostic texts like the *Gospel of Mary* (page 88) elevate women's roles and veneration of the feminine. All of these are valuable for understanding the role of women across the history of patriarchal religions.

Apocrypha offer these and other glimpses into the beliefs and practices of many Jews and Christians across history. I hope this book will help those who seek to understand perspectives beyond their own.

As Jesus says in the *Gospel of Thomas* (page 73), "Let one who seeks not stop seeking until one finds. When one finds, one will be troubled. When one is troubled, one will marvel and reign over all."

CHAPTER TWO

The Second Canon

This chapter will explore works that are considered "deuterocanonical," or part of a "second canon," set apart as "The Apocrypha" in certain Bibles or omitted completely. These works were all written in the Second Temple period. Alexander the Great's conquest of the Palestinian region in the fourth century BCE brought about many changes for the Jewish people as they were colonized under Greek rule. In this time of diaspora for the Jewish people, many emigrated from the Palestinian region to other areas like Egypt—which was also conquered by Alexander the Great and "Hellenized," or influenced by Greek culture, religion, and language.

The period brought about a flourishing of literature, much of it addressing anxieties about Jewish identity, observance of Israelite laws, living under empire, and diaspora. Some pieces of the Hebrew Bible (like the Torah, or Pentateuch) reached their final forms as we know them in this period. Other works included in the Hebrew Bible (like Ezra–Nehemiah, Esther, and Daniel) were composed in this period in response to the earlier Babylonian exile and its consequences.

Deuterocanonical books have remained part of Jewish and Christian traditions continuously since the Second Temple period. All but a few were included in the Septuagint and taken over into Christian Bibles in the East, early Latin translations of the Septuagint, and Jerome's Latin Vulgate. Some Protestant Bibles—like certain copies of the *King James Version* (KJV) and the *New Revised Standard Version* (NRSV) include these books in a separate section labeled "The Apocrypha."

Tobit

FACTS

Author: Unknown, but likely a Jew living in diaspora

Date written: Between about 225 and 175 BCE

Language: Hebrew, Aramaic, or Greek, transmitted primarily in the Greek Septuagint version and translations from it

Canons: Beta Israel, Roman Catholic, Eastern Orthodox, Oriental Orthodox, Assyrian Church of the East

SUMMARY

When the narrative starts, Tobit is introduced as a righteous man living in Nineveh. He follows Israelite laws and is persecuted by the Ninevites for his zealousness in giving proper burials to Israelites slain in battle. One night, he sleeps outside and is blinded by bird droppings in his eyes, which leads to domestic drama with his wife. Meanwhile, in the region of Media, a young woman named Sarah, daughter of Raguel, is tormented by the demon of lust, Asmodeus, who kills every man betrothed to her—seven of them so far. Both Tobit and Sarah cry out to God. In response, God sends the angel Raphael to solve their troubles.

Tobit sends his son, Tobias, to Media to retrieve money left with a man named Gabael. Tobit meets Raphael the angel, disguised as a human, and takes him as a companion. During their journey, a fish attacks Tobias, and Raphael instructs him to catch the fish and keep its heart, liver, and gall. When they reach Media, Raphael instructs Tobias to stay with Raguel and ask for Sarah's hand in marriage because he is her closest kinsman (a common practice at the time, based on Israelite law). Learning about Sarah's persecution, Tobias is moved to fall in love with her. Raguel agrees to their marriage, although he prepares a grave for the young man. During the night of the wedding of Tobias and Sarah, Tobias (with Raphael's help) uses the fish's heart and liver to drive off the demon Asmodeus—whom Raphael pursues, shackles, and strangles. A wedding feast ensues.

Tobias and Raphael regain the money from Gabael and return with Sarah to Tobit. When they return, Tobias (again with Raphael's help) uses the fish's gall to restore Tobit's eyesight. Tobit receives a prophecy about the destruction of Nineveh and reveals it to Tobias before dying. The story ends with Tobias and his family returning to Media, where Tobias lives out the rest of his life.

ANALYSIS

This fictional story of Tobit is not unlike the story of Job in some of its structure and themes, especially the general message of God's faithfulness to his righteous followers in the midst of suffering. Written in a time of widespread emigration, the book would have appealed to Jewish audiences of the diaspora who had questions about why God lets bad things happen to good people amid persecution by foreign empires, as well as those struggling to observe Israelite laws without the temple. After all, with only one temple in Jerusalem, Jews who lived outside Judea could visit synagogues to pray and learn but were unable to participate in sacrifices at the temple that were mandated by Israelite law.

In many ways, this story is largely domestic, focused on two families brought together by marriage. It also underscores the righteousness of following Israelite laws and maintaining faith in God despite hardships. It is filled with fantastical elements (the demon and miracles) and humor (Raphael's disguise, episodes about the fish and the grave) that lend some levity to the dark subject matter. *Tobit* has been central to worship in Christian communities, as it features two songs of praise in chapter 8 and Tobit's song of praise in chapter 13—all three of which have been used as hymns. Similarly, since much of the book revolves around purity and marriage, passages from *Tobit* are often used in wedding ceremonies. Roman Catholic doctrine relies on this book concerning reverence for the dead and the intercession of angels.

Judith

FACTS

Author: Unknown, but likely a Hellenistic Jew living in diaspora somewhere, such as Alexandria

Date written: Probably between about 200 and 100 BCE

Language: Hebrew or Greek, transmitted primarily in the Greek Septuagint version and translations from it

Canons: Beta Israel, Roman Catholic, Eastern Orthodox, Oriental Orthodox, Assyrian Church of the East

SUMMARY

Judith is structured into roughly two halves. The first part (chapters 1–7) deals with the rise of the Assyrian threat to Israel, led by King Nebuchadnezzar's general Holofernes and his incursion into the Palestinian region. Holofernes and his army besiege a city named Bethulia for thirty-four days, and the people of the city weaken. Citizens of Bethulia chastise the city's elders for not submitting for peace, and the elders plan to surrender if God does not intervene.

The second part (chapters 8–16) focuses on the beautiful widow Judith, a strict adherent to Israelite law. She confronts the Bethulian elders and convinces them to allow her to enact her plan before submitting to Holofernes. Judith and her maidservant go to the Assyrian camp pretending to be defectors, and Holofernes welcomes them. After three days, Holofernes is intent upon seducing Judith and throws a feast. That night, Holofernes invites her to his private tent, and Judith plies him with more wine. Although Holofernes poses the threat of rape to Judith, she overcomes him while he is passed out drunk and beheads him with his own sword. She stashes his head in her handbag and steals away with her maid back to Bethulia.

In the morning, the Assyrians discover Holofernes dead and attack the city, but they are routed by the Bethulians and retreat for good. The narrative ends with Judith and the Bethulians visiting Jerusalem for ritual purification and sacrifices as they recommit themselves to observance of Israelite laws.

ANALYSIS

Judith seems on the surface like a historical book, but a number of inaccuracies, inconsistencies, and anachronisms point to the author's intention to write something more like historical fiction. For instance, Nebuchadnezzar is introduced as king of Assyria (not Babylon, which would be correct), most scholars believe there was never a city named Bethulia, and the overall narrative conflates a number of biblical stories and characters. In fact, many of these conflations indicate that the author sought to craft an allegory for Israelite history.

The book relates a story of ethnoreligious resistance against an invading empire, using the historical background of the Assyrian invasion of Israel centuries earlier to emphasize themes of resistance through religious purity, devotion, and prayer. In this way, it shares parallels with stories from the biblical books of Judges and Esther.

Like other deuterocanonical books (such as *1–2 Maccabees*; see pages 23 and 25), this narrative would have appealed to Hellenistic Jews living as colonized subjects under foreign rulers. For Christians, Judith has historically been viewed more as an allegorical figure of virtues like humility, justice, chastity, and purity.

Judith has been a popular subject for Christian artists—most notably, paintings of Judith beheading Holofernes by Michelangelo Merisi da Caravaggio, Orazio Gentileschi, and his daughter, Artemisia Gentileschi.

Baruch

FACTS

Also known as: 1 *Baruch,* to distinguish it from a later apocryphon known as *2 Baruch*

Author: Unknown, but likely a Jew living in diaspora; attributed to Baruch, son of Neriah, scribe of the prophet Jeremiah

Date written: Probably between about 200 and 100 BCE

Language: Hebrew, Aramaic, or Greek, transmitted primarily in the Greek Septuagint version and translations from it

Canons: Beta Israel, Roman Catholic, Eastern Orthodox, Oriental Orthodox, Assyrian Church of the East

SUMMARY

Baruch is a composite work, stylized as a book of prophetic wisdom, compiled from earlier parts brought together. The book may be divided into roughly five main sections: an introduction, a confessional prayer about exile, a poem about wisdom, a poem about the restoration of Zion, and the Letter of Jeremiah. The final chapter, comprising the Letter of Jeremiah (a separate book in the Eastern Orthodox canon), is stylized as a letter from the eponymous prophet to the Israelites just before their captivity in Babylon under Nebuchadnezzar.

ANALYSIS

While this work is composite, the unifying theme of all of the sections is an extended meditation on exile and desire for return. Overall, the book of *Baruch* presents several genres of literature found in the Hebrew Bible, from poetry to prophecy to a letter to the Israelites. It demonstrates a vast array of emotions, including remorse, lament, hope, and joy.

Like other deuterocanonical books, it dwells on the problem of exilic diaspora and the Jewish people's desire to return to the Palestinian region, especially Jerusalem. While the content of this work reflects on the Babylonian exile, it would have been fitting for audiences in the later Second Temple period when it was composed, when the Babylonian exile was an allegory for Jewish diaspora in general.

Wisdom of Ben Sira

FACTS

Also known as: Ecclesiasticus, Sirach, and Wisdom of Jesus the Son of Sirach

Author: Yeshua ben Eliezer ben Sira, a Hellenistic Jew living in the Palestinian region or possibly Alexandria. ("Ben" is Hebrew for "son of," so his name is sometimes anglicized as "Jesus son of Sirach.") His (unnamed) grandson translated it into Greek while living in Egypt.

Date written: Between about 196 and 175 BCE; translated into Greek around 132 BCE

Language: Hebrew, transmitted primarily in the Greek Septuagint version and translations from it

Canons: Beta Israel, Roman Catholic, Eastern Orthodox, Oriental Orthodox, Assyrian Church of the East

DISCOVERY

Although this book was known in Greek and Latin for centuries, in 1896, Solomon Schechter discovered the Hebrew version among the Cairo Geniza collection of Jewish texts preserved at an Egyptian synagogue. Fragments of this work in that collection were copied in the eleventh and twelfth centuries but represent a much earlier version of the work—likely the one behind the Greek translation in the Septuagint.

SUMMARY

The *Wisdom of Ben Sira* is a large compilation of wisdom ranging across subjects and themes found in other Hebrew wisdom literature. It begins with an informative prologue by Ben Sira's grandson that tells us about Ben Sira's learning in the Torah, Prophets, and other Hebrew works; his composition of the book as a repository of wisdom; and his grandson's translation of the book into Greek.

The rest of the book is structured into roughly two halves (chapters 1–23 and 24–51), with each of these parts beginning with a poem about Wisdom personified. The contents of both major sections address reflections on many subjects like the Torah, practical advice, ethical teachings, theodicy, death, sin, social justice, women, eschatology, doxological praise of God, and salvation history. Some representative verses include discussions of wealth, generosity, and stinginess (14:3–8); the happiness of a man with a good wife (chapter 26); praise of almsgiving (29:9–13); and the difficulty of life and fear of death for all, from rich kings to the lowly poor (40:3–5). Notably, chapters 44–50 relate Israel's history in the form of praise of major Israelite heroes. It concludes with Ben Sira naming himself as the author, followed by a hymn of thanksgiving and a final poem about his lifelong search for wisdom.

ANALYSIS

Significantly, while most apocrypha remain anonymous, the *Wisdom of Ben Sira* is written by a known, identified author.

We know quite a bit about Ben Sira and his composition of this book compared to many other apocrypha (relatively speaking). In part, this is because Ben Sira and his grandson provide explicit information about themselves within the work itself. The prologue by Ben Sira's grandson is important as early evidence of some type of canonical status for the Torah and prophets of the Hebrew Bible. This prologue upholds learning and wisdom as necessary pursuits.

This book is especially aligned with biblical wisdom literature, an ancient genre (regularly in poetic form) that collects teachings about life and philosophical ideals often attributed to the sayings of great sages. In fact, Wisdom is personified throughout this book as a divine figure. Many of the same types of subjects in this book are found in Proverbs and Ecclesiastes, and it shares many similarities with those biblical books.

As already indicated in the summary, the contents cover many subjects, but consistent themes include the fear of God, the search for wisdom, adherence to the Torah, and salvation. It differs from Proverbs and Ecclesiastes in its intense focus on Israelite history and laws of the Torah. There is also a certain amount of influence from Hellenistic philosophical and intellectual ideals, like a systemic interest in human relationships and implications for living an ethical life.

1 Maccabees

FACTS

Author:	Unknown, but likely a Jew living in the Palestinian region
Date written:	Between 104 and 63 BCE
Language:	Hebrew, transmitted primarily in the Greek Septuagint version and translations from it
Canons:	Roman Catholic, Eastern Orthodox, Oriental Orthodox (excepting Orthodox Tewahedo), Assyrian Church of the East

SUMMARY

One of the two most important sources for the history of Israel between 174 and 134 BCE is *1 Maccabees*. Its main subject matter is the Maccabean Revolt, undertaken by the Jewish people against the imperial Greek ruler Antiochus IV Epiphanes, who in 167 BCE captured Jerusalem, desecrated the temple, slaughtered many Jews, and suppressed Jewish observation of Israelite laws in order to exert his control. All of this is part of the more general historical conquest of the Palestinian region by Alexander the Great and his successors, and the Hellenization of the Jewish people in the Second Temple period.

The majority of this historical book focuses on the exploits of the priest Mattathias and his sons. In response to Antiochus's actions, Mattathias urges his sons (John, Simon, Judas, Eleazar, and Jonathan) to rise up against the tyrant. Under the leadership of his son Judas Maccabeus ("the Hammer"), the Jewish people mount a militant revolt.

Much of the book is an account of Judas's experience heading the revolt. In his first battle, Judas leads a small, hungry band of men against a much larger Syrian army, which, after a rousing speech, he easily defeats. In another decisive battle, Antiochus employs armored elephants, made drunk and enraged on wine. One of Judas's men, Eleazar Avaran, runs into the midst of the elephants, identifies a weak spot in the armor of one of the beasts, and kills it by stabbing it. As the elephant falls, it lands on Eleazar and crushes him. Nonetheless, Judas and his army are victorious in this battle and many others because of these sorts of heroic deeds.

Eventually, Judas defeats Antiochus (in 165 BCE), frees the temple, and reinstates observance of Israelite laws. After Judas and his brothers cleanse the temple and make sacrifices, the Jewish people celebrate for eight days. This resulted in the establishment of the festival of Hanukkah every year. Judas then forms an alliance with the Romans in an attempt to oust the Greeks from control over the Palestinian region.

After Judas dies in battle, the rest of the history recounts the exploits of his brothers and their sons. Jonathan succeeds his brother as the leader of the revolt, and he is eventually appointed high priest. Jonathan is captured, and Simon undertakes leadership; he later appoints his own sons as leaders. However, Simon and his sons, Judas and Mattathias, are betrayed and murdered (in 134 BCE). Another of his sons, John Hyrcanus, takes up leadership, marking the beginning of the Hasmonean dynasty, which ruled over Judea semi-autonomously from the Greeks from 134 to around 116 BCE.

ANALYSIS

While it is a historical book, *1 Maccabees* is not a chronicle but a narrative. Like all historical accounts, it is shot through with the author's own agenda—in this case, a religious history of resistance by the Jewish people to encroaching Hellenism. Still, the historical account is generally reliable and has been corroborated by other evidence from the period. It is, therefore, a significant written source for the history of the Palestinian region in the second century.

It is also a national history about the Jewish people's need to return to Israelite laws and customs as a response to the divine punishment of imperial persecution for Jewish sins. It similarly presents propaganda about the establishment of the Hasmonean dynasty and in celebration of the heroism of the Hasmonean family (Mattathias, Judas, and his brothers). Judas's alliance with the Romans demonstrates the significance of their rise to power around the Mediterranean world and their rivalry with the Greeks.

2 Maccabees

FACTS

Author: Unknown, but likely a Jew living in the Palestinian region; condensed from a lost five-volume history by a Hellenistic Jew named Jason of Cyrene

Date written: Between 104 and 63 BCE

Language:	Greek, transmitted primarily in the Greek Septuagint version and translations from it
Canons:	Roman Catholic, Eastern Orthodox, Oriental Orthodox (excepting Orthodox Tewahedo), Assyrian Church of the East

SUMMARY

The other most important source for the history of Israel between 174 and 134 BCE is *2 Maccabees*. Like *1 Maccabees*, the main subject matter is the Maccabean Revolt; it is not a sequel but another account of the same events. Yet its focus, perspective, chronological scope, and agenda are different. In fact, it is a condensed version (an "epitome") of a five-volume history undertaken by Jason of Cyrene, adapted into this form by an anonymous Jewish compiler.

Rather than a history focused on the family of Judas Maccabeus and concluding with the creation of the Hasmonean dynasty, *2 Maccabees* is more focused on the temple in Jerusalem. It spends more time devoted to the lead-up to Antiochus's defamation of the temple and the deaths of the martyrs because of his tyranny. The narrative does feature Judas in its second half, but the rest of his family (Mattathias and his brothers) are largely absent. The history concludes with Judas leading the Jewish people in their victory over the Seleucid general Nicanor, resulting in the Jewish people reclaiming the temple and reinstating observance of Israelite laws.

ANALYSIS

The author's major focus is on Hellenization and threats because of encroaching Greek rulers and the Jewish people abandoning the Law. Events leading up to the Maccabean Revolt are interpreted as divine judgment, with the death of the martyrs as the climax of persecution for sins. The revolt is then imagined as a turning point toward reform.

The history includes several moments of supernatural events, like heavenly apparitions and divine interventions that are meant to sanctify the actions of the Jewish people in their revolt. Among these, the narrative is often sensationalized, especially with intense portrayals of violence. Theological reflections also appear in this book, like ideas about bodily resurrection (as for the martyrs) that developed in the Second Temple period and were a part of Judaism during the time of Jesus.

Wisdom of Solomon

FACTS

Also known as: Wisdom, Book of Wisdom
Author: Unknown, but likely a Hellenistic Jew living in diaspora in Egypt, probably in Alexandria; attributed to King Solomon
Date written: Between about 50 BCE and 50 CE
Language: Greek, transmitted primarily in the Greek Septuagint version and translations from it
Canons: Roman Catholic, Eastern Orthodox, Oriental Orthodox, Assyrian Church of the East

SUMMARY

The *Wisdom of Solomon* is a reflection on seeking Wisdom, personified as a divine figure, for living a righteous life, and eternal consequences. The author evokes several details about King Solomon in a first-person prayer in chapter 9, which is why it has traditionally been attributed to him and aligned with the biblical books of Proverbs and Ecclesiastes. The book is structured in three major parts. The first part (chapters 1–5) focuses on Wisdom and eschatology, or human destiny after death, concerned with good and evil, judgment, and eternal consequences. The second part (chapters 6–9) focuses on the origin and nature of Wisdom, concerned with the quest for Wisdom in life. The third (chapters 10–19) focuses on Wisdom in Israelite history, concerned with the role of Wisdom in Israel's salvation.

ANALYSIS

This work synthesizes Hebrew wisdom, Greek philosophy, and Hellenistic literature. While it is a work of ideas about wisdom, much of the book draws on apocalyptic literature, especially in its reflections on eschatology and the afterlife. (See chapter 8 for more on this type of literature.) A common theme through all of the sections, then, is the relationship between judgment and salvation. At the same time, while this theme is rooted in Jewish ideas, the synthetic nature of the book and exhortations throughout indicate that the author might have intended it for a mixed audience of Jews and non-Jews alike. Such attention to a mixed audience would have been relevant for a Jewish author living in diaspora in Egypt, where he would have interacted with many non-Jewish members of the community.

Additions to Esther

FACTS

Author: Unknown, but likely a Hellenistic Jew living in diaspora in Egypt, probably in Alexandria; attributed to Lysimachus, son of Ptolemy

Date written: Around 77 BCE

Language: Greek, transmitted primarily in the Greek Septuagint version and translations from it

Canons: Roman Catholic, Eastern Orthodox, Oriental Orthodox, Assyrian Church of the East

SUMMARY

The biblical book of Esther features a young Israelite woman in Persia who becomes queen by marrying King Ahasuerus (Xerxes I, also known as Artaxerxes I). She then has to petition her husband in order to stop a plot by the evil viceroy Haman to commit genocide against the Jewish people. When the Hebrew book of Esther was translated into Greek in the first century BCE, the translator included a number of additions (probably composed by the translator). These include an introduction and a visionary dream of Mordecai, Esther's cousin; a version of the decree by King Ahasuerus against the Jews; prayers by Mordecai and Esther; an expanded account of Esther before the king and direct mention of God's intervention; a version of Ahasuerus's decree in favor of the Jews; Mordecai's interpretation of his dream in relation to the events of the story; and, at the end, a colophon that identifies Lysimachus, son of Ptolemy, as the translator of the book into Greek.

ANALYSIS

In many ways, the additions to Esther add elements of other genres from biblical and early Jewish literature. Mordecai's dream and his later interpretation of it related to the events of the story align him with other prophetic figures in the Hebrew Bible, including Joseph and Daniel. Versions of Artaxerxes's two decrees add historical features to the narrative as well as lend authority. Prayers by Mordecai and Esther as well as the note about God's intervention add a religious element lacking in the original narrative (which, along with Song of Songs, is one of the only two books in the Bible that never actually mentions God) and the prayers align with others in the Hebrew Bible. Esther before the king increases dramatic and emotional aspects of the story in a key moment of climatic suspense. Taken together, these additions are interspersed throughout the narrative in order to fill in details not in the Hebrew book, shifting some of the narrative emphasis to highlight the salvation of the Jewish people through religious redemption.

Additions to Daniel

FACTS

Author: Unknown, compiled by a Hellenistic Jew living in diaspora, probably in Alexandria

Date written: Second Temple period, by around 100 BCE

Language: Hebrew, Aramaic, and Greek, transmitted primarily in the Greek Septuagint version and translations from it

Canons: Roman Catholic, Eastern Orthodox, Oriental Orthodox, Assyrian Church of the East

SUMMARY

When the book of Daniel was translated into Greek around 100 BCE, the translator included a number of additions. These include two narratives and two hymns: Susanna and the Elders, Bel and the Dragon, and The Prayer of Azariah and Song of the Three Children.

The first two might be considered some of the earliest works of detective fiction, featuring courtroom intrigue, mystery puzzles, and prison drama. In Susanna and the Elders, Susanna is introduced as a virtuous, beautiful young woman married to Joakim, a rich, well-respected man. One day, two elders who have been appointed as judges see Susanna walking in her husband's gardens and begin to lust after her. They wait until she is alone in the garden bathing and try to coerce her into sleeping with them. She refuses, so they accuse her of being with a man who is not her husband and take her to court. She is condemned based on the judges' false testimony and sentenced to death for adultery.

But Daniel (the same Daniel who in the Bible survived the lions' den and read the writing on the wall) intervenes. He separates the two judges and cross-examines them. When they give different answers to the same questions, he deduces that they are lying and sentences them to death.

Bel and the Dragon contains two narrative episodes, both reminiscent of stories in the canonical book of Daniel. In the first, Daniel refuses to worship an idol of a god named Bel, and King Cyrus challenges him to prove that the god is false, believing it must be real because it always eats food left for it as a sacrifice. Daniel instructs Cyrus to leave food in the temple and lock it so no one can come eat it at night. But the priests have a hidden entrance and sneak in with their families to eat the food overnight. In the morning, Cyrus shows Daniel the empty sanctuary and condemns the prophet to death. Daniel, however, had sprinkled ashes on the floor, making the priests' footprints visible. He reveals a trapdoor, and Cyrus puts the priests and their families to death.

In the second episode, Daniel challenges the authenticity of an idol of a great dragon by feeding it a homemade concoction of food, causing the dragon to burst open. Although Daniel reveals the dragon idol to be a false god, the Babylonians pressure the king to punish him anyway. Daniel is thrown into a lions' den for six days. Meanwhile, far away in Judea, an angel visits the prophet Habakkuk, grabs him by the top of his head, and transports him to Babylon to feed Daniel. On the seventh day, the king opens the lions' den and finds Daniel safe and sound. In turn, he throws the men who plotted against Daniel into the lions' den, where they are devoured.

The two hymns include blessings and supplications for God's salvation, sung by Shadrach, Meshach, and Abednego, the three youths thrown into the fiery furnace in Daniel 3.

ANALYSIS

Many apocrypha about Daniel were composed in the Second Temple, late antique, and medieval periods; those included in the Septuagint version of Daniel are only representatives of dozens of others. The additions presented here were not composed by the translator of Daniel but existed before and were added to the longer book. The narratives were independent, while the two songs were probably part of early Jewish worship in the Second Temple era. Like other aspects of the book of Daniel, these added stories revolve around themes of virtue and piety in the face of villainy and persecution.

The story about Susanna revolves around the complexity of Israelite laws and criticizes the religious establishment of judges, probably as a satire on priests and authorities of the time. Episodes about Bel and the Dragon emphasize resisting outside influences and adherence to Israelite laws in the face of pagan religious pressures. Overall, these additions drive home the main theme of Daniel about God's deliverance of those who remain righteous in the face of persecution.

Additional Second Canon Texts

PSALM 151

Psalm 151 was composed sometime during the Second Temple period (before about 200 BCE) by an unknown author. Although originally written in Hebrew, it was transmitted primarily through the Greek version in the Septuagint. Attributed to King David, it relates his life as a poet and his victory over Goliath from a first-person perspective. Today it is considered canonical in the Eastern Orthodox Church, Oriental Orthodox Church, and Assyrian Church of the East.

PRAYER OF MANASSEH

The *Prayer of Manasseh* was composed in Greek between about 100 BCE and 100 CE by either a Jewish or early Christian author. Attributed to Manasseh, king of Judah (697–643 BCE), it is stylized as a prayer of penitence for his idolatry. Structurally, it includes three parts, including praise of God, confession for sins, and supplication for forgiveness. Today it is considered canonical in the Eastern Orthodox Church, Oriental Orthodox Church, and Assyrian Church of the East.

CHAPTER THREE

Apocrypha of the Hebrew Bible

Jewish literature flourished in the postbiblical periods, with a whole host of apocryphal literature emerging during the Second Temple, late antique, and medieval eras. This chapter discusses some of the most prominent of these works. Many of these apocrypha share some of the same themes and literary concerns as the deutero-canonical books and were composed in many cases around the same time. Certain of these works may be seen as midrashic, or meant to fill in details and explain aspects of the Hebrew Bible.

Several of these apocrypha are particularly important for the history of Christianity because they were adopted into Christian biblical canons. For example, *Jubilees* is accepted by Orthodox Tewahedo Christians; *3 Maccabees* is part of the canon accepted by Eastern Orthodox, Syriac Orthodox, and Assyrian Church of the East communities; and *4 Maccabees* is accepted by Eastern Orthodox Christians. In some cases, like *Jubilees* and *Joseph and Aseneth*, even when they were not considered canonical, they were widespread and popular among Christians.

Although most of the books discussed in this chapter were composed by Jewish authors, recent scholarship recognizes that some (like the *Life of Adam and Eve* and *Joseph and Aseneth*) might have been composed or at least adapted into the forms we know by Christian authors.

Life of Adam and Eve

FACTS

Also known as: *Apocalypse of Moses* (Greek), *Vita Adae et Evae* (Latin), *Penitence of Adam* (Armenian), *Book of Adam* (Georgian)

Author: Unknown; probably an early Christian, but possibly a Hellenistic Jew

Date written: Between about 100 and 600 CE

Language: Probably originally in Greek, but the longer version survives in Latin, Armenian, and Georgian

Canons: None, but popular in various Christian communities

DISCOVERY

The first modern publication of this work was Constantin von Tischendorf's edition of the Greek shorter version in 1866. Wilhelm Meyer published the first edition of the Latin longer version in 1878, and Victor Jagic published the first edition of the Church Slavic longer version in 1893. Since these publications, dozens of new manuscripts have been discovered of different versions in Greek, Latin, Armenian, Georgian, and Church Slavic, and fragments in Coptic have been found.

SUMMARY

The *Life of Adam and Eve* takes Genesis 3 as its starting point and expands the biblical narrative with a much fuller account of Adam and Eve's story after their expulsion from the Garden of Eden.

Specific contents vary across different versions, so this summary deals with the longer narrative. Driven from the garden, Adam and Eve search in vain for food, so they resort to acts of penitence such as standing in the Jordan River for forty days. Satan appears as an angel and deceives Eve again, then when questioned he recounts that he and other angels were cast out of heaven for not venerating Adam as the image of God.

The second half of the narrative concerns Adam and Eve's children, first Cain and Abel and then Seth. Adam relates to Seth a revelation of secret knowledge about when he was taken up into heavenly paradise and saw the angels worshipping God. Adam then falls ill and recounts the story of his and Eve's fall. Seth and Eve journey to the Garden of Eden and Seth is bitten by a serpent, whom Eve curses and Seth rebukes. Seth receives the oil of the tree of mercy from an angel, and he and Eve return with spices. Adam then dies, and for seven days the sun, moon, and stars darken while Eve and Seth mourn. Eve senses her own death coming, instructs her children to create tablets of stone and clay relating Adam's and her life, and then dies. The narrative ends with a brief appendix relating Seth's creation of the tablets, their discovery after the Flood, and Solomon reading them.

ANALYSIS

The *Life of Adam and Eve* is mainly a midrashic exposition of the lives of the title characters after their expulsion from the Garden of Eden. It provides a greatly expanded narrative about the post-Edenic fate of Adam, Eve, and Seth in more detail than Genesis. At the same time, it provides a classic explanation of ideas about the relationship between the serpent and Satan as well as Satan's background, which developed in Second Temple writings. The work is one of many that identifies the serpent, Satan, and the fallen angel, Lucifer, in a developing mythology around the figure. It also provides information to juxtapose the early Paradise (Eden) with the heavenly Paradise in eschatological terms (concerning death and the afterlife).

Different versions across languages present a complicated web of interrelated texts. In fact, scholars often talk about the different texts as separate compositions. Some scholars have proposed Hebrew as the original language, but no evidence of a Hebrew text has been discovered, and most scholars now agree that Greek was the original language. Even more complicated, the various versions survive only in Christian manuscripts, with Christian influences in the text (maybe interpolated, or added later), so it is unclear whether the original and adaptations were composed by Jewish or Christian authors.

Jubilees

FACTS

Also known as: Designated "The Little Genesis" in some witnesses

Author: An unknown Jewish reformer living in the Palestinian region; attributed to Moses

Date written: Between about 160 and 140 BCE

Language: It survives in full form only in Geʻez, but copies of parts of the book found among the Dead Sea Scrolls provided scholars with new information about its origins. It was likely composed in Hebrew, then translated into Greek, and then into Geʻez (from Greek).

Canons: Beta Israel, Orthodox Tewahedo

SUMMARY

Jubilees is a rewritten adaptation of Genesis and Exodus 1–12, often with passages from the biblical books incorporated. It begins by claiming to have been given as a revelation by an angel of God to Moses on Mount Sinai. In general, the author follows the narrative of Israel's history in the first two books of the Hebrew Bible, including stories about creation, Adam and Eve, Noah and the Flood, Abraham, Jacob (the central figure of the book), and Moses. Yet the author omits, expands, and elaborates many aspects of these stories. Notable expansions to the biblical narrative include explanations of the prohibition on nakedness in relation to Adam and Eve; feasts associated with the flood and God's covenant; Abraham's sacrifice of Isaac; the dispute between Jacob and Esau turning into a war; and the actions of angels and demons. For example, the first verses of Genesis 6 are expanded with a narrative that explains the Flood as punishment for humans fornicating with a group of angels in the form of giants, leading to human corruption, cannibalism, and evil.

Some of the additions are particularly humanizing moments. For instance, as a young man, Abram (later Abraham) is especially pious and advocates against idolatry, eventually burning the family idols; his father, Haran, rushes in to save the idols and dies in the fire. The death of Abraham is particularly striking: at the Feast of Firstfruits, he calls his young grandson Jacob to him and gives a series of blessings to the boy before they fall asleep together, with Jacob resting on Abraham's chest as the patriarch dies in his sleep.

After Abraham's death (chapter 23), there is an extended apocalyptic vision of Israel's history, emphasizing God's covenant, sin, punishment, repentance, and salvation. After relating Moses's life, the book ends with extended legal explanations about observing Passover, Jubilees, and the Sabbath.

ANALYSIS

The likeliest reason for the composition of *Jubilees* was to promote religious reform. In the face of increasing Hellenization during the Second Temple era, reformers sought a return to traditional interpretations and adherence to Israelite laws. Throughout this work, the author emphasizes Israel's relationship to God, adherence to Israelite laws, concerns about women (Israelite and foreign), eschatological themes, messianism, and attention to calendrical time. The last is a special appeal to calculate time according to a solar calendar, rather than the standard Jewish lunar calendar, with an emphasis on a measurement in "jubilees" (a symbolic unit of time)—hence the title of the book. Many of the expansions of the biblical stories offer explanations like commentaries that spell out a way of life based on "halacha," or Israelite laws. In this way, the book is a lot like Jewish Midrash, or commentary on Hebrew scriptures.

There is also an intense interest in supernatural elements like angels and demons. Because of this interest and a particular focus on the figure of Enoch, the work shares connections with *1 Enoch* (see page 114) as well as other early Jewish apocalyptic literature. The conclusion especially highlights the significance of observing the Jewish sabbath and feasts as necessary for following Israelite laws.

Joseph and Aseneth

FACTS

Author: Unknown; probably an early Christian, but possibly a Hellenistic Jew

Date written: Between about 100 BCE and 400 CE

Language: Greek; but it also survives in Armenian, Ge'ez, Latin, Church Slavic, and Syriac

Canons: Not part of any canon, but popular in various Christian communities, especially in Eastern Orthodox Christianity

SUMMARY

In the canonical book of Genesis, Joseph marries Aseneth, the daughter of an Egyptian priest. *Joseph and Aseneth* is a historical fiction that expands their love story. Aseneth is presented as a beautiful virgin pursued by many suitors, including Pharaoh's son, all of whom she spurns. Joseph, who (as in Genesis) has already become

Pharaoh's vital aide, requests a visit with Pentepheres, an Egyptian priest who is Aseneth's father. Before Joseph enters, Pentepheres suggests to Aseneth that he will give her to Joseph for marriage. She refuses, but then falls in love with Joseph at first sight when he visits. Joseph wants nothing to do with her, because as the daughter of an Egyptian priest, she worships false idols. Greatly distressed, Aseneth returns to her tower, fasts for seven days, repents, destroys her idols, and converts. God sends an angel to comfort her, and Joseph accepts her as his bride.

After Aseneth meets Joseph's family, the story transitions to the next part of the narrative, eight years later. Pharaoh's son sees Aseneth again, and his lust for her (from when he was one of her suitors) is rekindled. He plots to murder Joseph and kidnap Aseneth, but he is thwarted and killed by Joseph's brothers Simeon, Levi, and Benjamin (the same brothers who sold Joseph into slavery out of jealousy). Pharaoh dies after this plot, and Joseph becomes ruler of Egypt.

ANALYSIS

Circumstances of the work's survival and transmission raise serious questions about its origins. While scholars previously believed that it was a Jewish work that was later taken over by Christians, more scholars now believe that it was composed by an early Christian. This has led to controversial interpretations, as journalist Simcha Jacobovici and Professor Barrie Wilson have claimed that the work is an early Christian "lost gospel," composed as an allegorical story about Jesus's marriage to Mary Magdalene. Many scholars have critiqued this interpretation for its surface-level reading and the sensationalized story behind it, rather than measured analysis.

A more accepted explanation is that this work tackles a major question of anxiety for early interpreters of Genesis: How can Joseph's role in the salvation history of the chosen people of Israel and his marriage to a foreign woman and daughter of an Egyptian priest be reconciled? Aseneth is famed for her beauty and virginity, and in her description she is compared to Israelite women like Sarah, Rebecca, and Rachel. From the start, this establishes anxiety about her status as a non-Israelite partner for Joseph. Yet any anxieties are resolved by Aseneth's lengthy conversion and interactions with the angel of God. The plotline likely addressed contemporary audiences (Jewish, Christian, or both) concerned with intermarriage and conversion. These anxieties would have been particularly appropriate in a time when Jews, Christians, and Jewish Christians were increasingly in contact with outsiders who identified with other religious beliefs.

3 Maccabees

FACTS

Author:	An unknown Hellenistic Jew living in diaspora in Egypt, probably in Alexandria
Date written:	Between about 100 and 30 BCE
Language:	Greek
Canons:	Eastern Orthodox, Syriac Orthodox, Assyrian Church of the East; it appears in manuscripts of the Septuagint such as the Codex Alexandrinus and Codex Venetus

SUMMARY

Despite its title, and some overlapping story elements, this book is not related to *1–2 Maccabees* and does not concern events related to the Maccabean Revolt. Instead, it is focused on the persecution of the Jewish people by Ptolemy IV Philopator (a Hellenistic king of Egypt), who ruled from 221 to 204 BCE, well before the Maccabean Revolt. Much of the book, however, is legendary rather than historical.

The work begins abruptly in the middle of the Battle of Raphia (217 BCE) waged between Philopator and the Seleucid Antiochus

III the Great as part of the Syrian Wars. Victorious, Ptolemy visits nearby Jerusalem, where he learns that only the high priest can enter the innermost sanctuary of the temple. He enters it himself, but God, hearing the high priest's prayers, stops Ptolemy by temporarily paralyzing him. Ptolemy returns to his capital of Alexandria, outraged by the incident; in retaliation, he rounds up the Jews in a horse-racing stadium to face death. His attempts to kill the Jews are continually thwarted by divine intervention, as God makes him fall asleep at inopportune times or take back his execution orders and then forget he did so. This culminates in an episode where Ptolemy personally leads 500 intoxicated elephants to the stadium to trample the Jews to death—but, in response to the prayers of a virtuous Jewish man named Eleazar, God sends two angels, who turn the elephants against the king's own forces.

In the end, Ptolemy forgets his anger against the Jews, throws a feast for them, issues a decree in their favor, and lets them return home safe and sound.

ANALYSIS

While this book is more like a work of historical fiction, *3 Maccabees* shares many of the same elements as *1–2 Maccabees*. It overlaps with *Against Apion*, a work by first-century Jewish-Roman historian Flavius Josephus, which relates some of the same legend. Foremost are the themes of persecution and resistance, especially in the face of empire and Hellenization encroaching on early Jewish culture. In fact, the author uses this story of the past as a sort of ideological allegory to promote Jewish resistance to the Romans and Egyptians in power at the time.

Instead of militant revolt, the book emphasizes piety and martyrdom as resistance. In this, there are similarities with the portrayal of martyrdom in *2 Maccabees* 6–7. Through all of this, the Jews are depicted as having special status as God's chosen people, which gives them a certain amount of protection. Since it was composed in Egypt, about an Egyptian ruler, there are certainly layers of social commentary that would appeal to Jews living in diaspora. Those disillusioned with Egyptian rule would have appreciated the satirical elements critical of Ptolemy that set him up as thwarted by God's interventions.

4 Maccabees

FACTS

Author: An unknown Hellenistic Jew living in diaspora, possibly in Syrian Antioch; sometimes attributed to Josephus
Date written: Between 63 BCE and 38 CE
Language: Greek
Canons: Eastern Orthodox; it appears in manuscripts of the Septuagint such as the Codex Sinaiticus, Codex Alexandrinus, and Codex Venetus

SUMMARY

4 Maccabees takes its starting point from the story of the Jewish martyrs as in *2 Maccabees* 6–7, but it is mainly a philosophical work. The first section lays out a philosophical reflection on the superiority of reason over passion. As cases to support his points, the author uses examples from the Hebrew Bible, including Joseph, Moses, Jacob, and David. For example, Moses is cited as using his reason to moderate his anger with Dathan and Abiram for rebelling against him. David is upheld as governing his passions when he encountered grave thirst but, when he found water, he poured it out as a libation to God out of piety.

The second section, the main portion of the work, discusses in detail the martyrdom of Eleazar, his seven brothers, and their mother. The author provides detailed descriptions of their martyrdoms and speeches. Eleazar is stripped, bound, and whipped in an attempt to force him to recant his faith, but he holds true, as the author says, because of his reason. Next, the first brother is stripped, whipped, and then put upon a torture wheel until his limbs break; the other six brothers are put on similar machines, which tear their bodies apart as told in gory detail. The brothers, like Eleazar, stand firm in reason and denounce the king instead of God. What follows is a "panegyric," or formal praise, for their mother, who dies by suicide to escape defilement (an act of reason according to the Stoics), and she is upheld as the greatest example of reason over passions. The book ends with an account of the mother's address to her children and a celebration of divine justice for the righteous.

ANALYSIS

This work is one of philosophy more than most others discussed in this book. It is, most basically, a synthesis of Hellenistic philosophy through a framework of Jewish adherence to the Torah. While the author adopts aspects of Platonism and Stoicism, the core of this book is clearly a Jewish religious outlook informed by Israelite laws. This synthesis is somewhat ironic, given that the author is steeped in Greek philosophy even as he seeks to uphold Jewish Torah in resistance to Hellenization.

As with *2 Maccabees* and *3 Maccabees*, there is a concern with martyrdom in the face of empire, Hellenization, and persecution. Persecution and martyrdom are even more pronounced in this book, since the main narrative dwells upon detailed scenes of intense, violent martyrdom. The goal, however, is to uphold reason in the face of violence—for the characters as well as readers. Like the earlier books of Maccabees, this book is concerned with resistance, though instead of emphasizing militant revolt or martyrdom, it foregrounds philosophical reason as the framework and intelligence, self-control, justice, and courage as the means. Again, there is some irony in all of this, considering the author's rhetorical flourishes through violent imagery of martyrdom meant to inspire passion as a way to lead toward reason.

Alphabet of Ben Sira

FACTS

Author: Unknown; attributed to Joshua (Jesus) ben ("son of") Eliezer ben Sira (see *Wisdom of Ben Sira*, page 21)

Date written: Between about 700 and 1000 CE, probably in or around Iraq

Language: Hebrew and Aramaic

Canons: None

DISCOVERY

This work circulated in medieval manuscripts in Europe and the Near East. It has also been relatively well-known to scholars of Jewish literature in modern times. It was published early in the era of print, in Thessaloniki in 1514, Constantinople in 1519, and Venice in 1544.

SUMMARY

The *Alphabet of Ben Sira* is a parody of Hebrew wisdom literature like the *Wisdom of Ben Sira* (attributed to the same figure). It is a composite work, made up of different genres often found in wisdom literature, but all within a humorous framework of mock-imitation of other such collections. The work survives in a few different versions, but the contents are generally the same.

The main framework of the *Alphabet* focuses on legends about Ben Sira, whose life is wholly fictionalized. The story of Ben Sira's "miraculous" conception begins the parodic narrative: The prophet Jeremiah is forced to masturbate in a bathhouse by antagonists and his semen is left floating in the waters when his daughter bathes, leading to her pregnancy. Because of Ben Sira's parentage and miraculous birth, he is a sort of wunderkind: precocious, more knowledgeable than his teachers, and a sage at the court of Nebuchadnezzar.

The rest of this work is made up of humorous expansions of biblical stories, proverbs, parables, and question-and-answer sequences. For example, Nebuchadnezzar asks Ben Sira a series of questions such as: "Why were farts created?"; "Why were mosquitoes created?"; "Why are the cat and the dog enemies?"; "Why does the raven copulate by mouth?"; and many more.

One of the most prominent expansions of the Bible concerns Lilith, presented as the first wife of Adam. When she is created, Lilith refuses to submit to Adam by lying beneath him during sex. This parodic domestic drama escalates in a dialogue about the equality of man and woman, until Lilith has had enough, speaks the Ineffable Name of God, and flies away. God sends angels to convince Lilith to return to Adam, but she refuses and accepts the consequence of becoming the mother of demons and seeing 100 of her children die every day.

ANALYSIS

As is already clear, the work is parody, infused with much humor despite its framework in the genre of wisdom literature like Jewish Midrash. In both details and its overall framework, the work satirizes the Bible, rabbinic authority, and Jewish literature. The *Alphabet* is humorous for more than entertainment, though; its composition and allusions are highly learned and likely reflect social satire about rabbinic traditions. In other words, the author must have been steeped in rabbinic learning and knowledgeable about rabbinic cultural norms, and probably was a student of Rabbinic Judaism. In turn, he used that learning both for satire and to uphold rabbinic identity. This work was popular throughout the medieval period but sometimes censored because of its ironic criticism of religion and rabbinic authority.

Book of Jasher

FACTS

Also known as: Sefer haYashar, Book of the Upright, Book of the Just
Author: Unknown
Date written: Unknown, before about 600 BCE
Language: Hebrew
Canons: None

SUMMARY

In the Hebrew Bible, both Joshua 10:13 and 2 Samuel 1:18 cite "the Book of Jasher." This is one of more than twenty books mentioned in the Hebrew Bible that were known to biblical authors but no longer survive.

Scholars believe that this book was a compilation of war poetry, like those recorded in the Hebrew Bible. The verse in Joshua is a celebration of when God routed the Ammonites, leading to the Israelites' victory. It is short enough to quote in full:

"Sun, stand still at Gibeon,
and Moon, in the valley of Aijalon."
And the sun stood still, and the moon stopped,
until the nation took vengeance on their enemies.
> **—Joshua 10:12–13 (NRSV)**

This is, presumably, an ancient Hebrew poetic description of the prolonged battle.

The poem recorded in 2 Samuel 1:19–27 is longer, as it relates David's dirge for King Saul and his son Jonathan after their deaths. The theme is found in the enduring refrain, "How the mighty have fallen" (vv. 19, 25, and 27), as it is an intense reflection on loss replete with military imagery. Just before the reference to "the

Book of Jasher," the text names this poem as "The Bow," often reconstructed as "Song of the Bow," and relates that David taught it to the people of Judah (v. 18).

These two sets of verses presumably give some sense of the types of poems included in the *Book of Jasher*.

ANALYSIS

The lost *Book of Jasher* is shrouded in mystery. Several apocrypha with this title have been published, and the major challenge is that none of these is a genuine work of prebiblical literature, probably none composed earlier than the medieval period.

One work, published in Venice in 1625 (though possibly from the high Middle Ages), relates biblical history from the creation of Adam to the Israelite conquest of Canaan, with many expansions and added stories about major figures like Noah, Abraham, and Moses. Another, now known as *Pseudo-Jasher*, was published in 1750 by Jacob Ilive (an English printer) and includes a title page claiming that it was translated by the eighth-century cleric Alcuin; it covers biblical history to the time of Jasher, son of Caleb (one of Moses's lieutenants), who is supposed to be the author. In 2003, the American science-fiction and fantasy author Benjamin Rosenbaum published a fictional translation of the lost Hebrew "Book of Jashar" in the speculative fiction magazine *Strange Horizons*. In addition to all of these, several other medieval Hebrew Jewish treatises have the title *Sefer haYashar*.

Still, all of these apocrypha are fascinating examples of how a tiny detail in the Bible sparked later authors to attempt to fill in and explain biblical narratives, as well as the fascinating subject of apocryphal fakes and forgeries from early Judaism to the present.

Additional Beta Israel and Orthodox Tewahedo Scriptures

Several other works related to or derived from Jewish literature are accepted in the Orthodox Tewahedo canon observed by Ethiopian Christians, some of which are also accepted by the Ethiopian Jewish community known as Beta Israel. These works are written in Ge'ez, an ancient Ethiopian language now used only in religious services and texts. (See also *1 Enoch* and *2 Esdras* in chapter 8.)

JOSIPPON

Also known as *Sefer Yosipon, Book of Joseph ben Gurion, Yoséf wäldä Koryon, Zena Ayhud* (*Story of the Jews*), and "another book of the Maccabees" (in the Ethiopian tradition), this work relates biblical history from Adam to the destruction of the Second Temple in 70 CE. It recounts events from the Hebrew Bible in relation to Babylonian, Greek, and Roman history. The anonymous author uses a variety of sources from antiquity but attributes his source to a history written by the real-life Jewish-Roman historian Josephus. It was originally written in Hebrew by a Greek-speaking Jew in southern Italy during the tenth century, and was translated into Ge'ez, probably from Greek, in the fourteenth century. Beta Israel considers this an important work of great influence, but not canonical.

1-3 MEQABYAN

Sometimes called the Ethiopian Maccabees (*Meqabyan*), these books are largely legendary accounts of the martyrdoms of three Jewish figures under the rule of a tyrannical king named Tsirutsaydan, whose name likely derives from the names of the cities of Tyre and Sidon ("*Tsur u Tsaydan*" in Ge'ez). At least some parts of these books are based on *Josippon*. The books include digressions relating theological concerns about the resurrection of the dead. The third book is less narrative and more of a reflection on salvation and punishment, with examples drawn from the Hebrew Bible, including the punishment the devil received for refusing to bow down to Adam, as in other apocrypha about Adam and in the Qur'an. These works were likely composed in the late fourteenth or early fifteenth century, but they are quoted in other works of the fifteenth and sixteenth century, so their reputation was established by that period. These works are also accepted as canonical by Beta Israel.

4 BARUCH

Also known as *Paralipomena of Baruch* or *Jeremiah*, *Säqoqawä Eremyas*, this work revolves around the destruction of Jerusalem by the Babylonians and the Israelite people's captivity and exile. It is attributed to Jeremiah in the Greek tradition but to Baruch in the Ethiopic tradition. It was originally composed in Hebrew, Aramaic, or possibly Greek between 70 and 136 CE and later translated into Ge'ez from Greek. This work is also accepted as canonical by Beta Israel.

CHAPTER FOUR

The Dead Sea Scrolls

I n the winter of 1946 or 1947, three young Bedouin shepherds were throwing rocks into a cave near the northwestern shore of the Dead Sea when they heard the sound of clay shattering. Hoping for treasure, they investigated and found what is perhaps the most significant modern discovery related to the Bible: the Dead Sea Scrolls.

Less than a mile away from the cave sit the ruins of a complex of buildings known as Qumran. In 1951, archaeological investigations of this site began, and scholars have since understood Qumran and the Dead Sea Scrolls as pieces of the same puzzle. In the following decades, archaeologists continued to excavate Qumran and surrounding areas. In total, they recovered thousands of fragments making up around 800 different documents from eleven caves. All of these came from a sectarian Jewish community (or related groups) that most scholars identify as the Essenes, who lived at and around Qumran between about 150 BCE and 68 CE.

This collection includes Hebrew, Aramaic, and Greek copies of books of the Hebrew Bible, deuterocanonical works, Jewish pseudepigrapha, biblical commentaries, astrological works, and rules governing the sectarian community's lifestyle. Among these are copies of *Tobit, Sirach, Jubilees, 1 Enoch*, and apocryphal psalms, as well as apocrypha featuring figures like Noah, Abraham, Joseph, Moses, Joshua, and Samuel. The Dead Sea Scrolls offer a substantial look at Jewish culture during the turbulent Second Temple period and contexts for Judaism during Jesus's life.

The story of the recovery and publication of the Dead Sea Scrolls is full of controversy and challenges spanning nearly fifty years. While some authors have benefited from popularizing sensationalized accounts and conspiracy theories about Vatican cover-ups, the realities are even more complicated. The process was hindered by the Israeli-Palestinian conflict, questions about who owns rights to the scrolls, controversies among academics, the slow nature of information dissemination before the Digital Age, and challenges of piecing together and analyzing the thousands of fragments that survive.

Over the years, many volumes of edited texts of the scrolls were published, but some were slow to make it to print. A full facsimile edition of photographs was published in 1991, breaking many barriers to research. Geza Vermes published an authoritative translation as *The Complete Dead Sea Scrolls in English* in 1997, while Martin Abegg, Jr., Peter Flint, and Eugene Ulrich published a translation of *The Dead Sea Scrolls Bible* in 1999. Now, photographs of the Dead Sea Scrolls are freely available to the public online via the Israel Antiquities Authority, at DeadSeaScrolls.org.il.

One thing to note in this chapter is that the Dead Sea Scrolls are designated with scroll titles based on which cave they were found in.

THE ESSENES AND THE DEAD SEA SCROLLS

Soon after the discovery of the Dead Sea Scrolls, scholars identified the authors as members of a Jewish sectarian group known as the Essenes. Most experts continue to hold this view. Who were the

Essenes, what do we know about them, and why do scholars identify them as the sect responsible for the Dead Sea Scrolls?

Before the discoveries around Qumran, evidence about the Essenes had been known to modern scholars largely because of early Jewish and Roman historians. The main accounts appear in works by the Jewish philosopher Philo of Alexandria (ca. 20 BCE–50 CE), the Roman author Pliny the Elder (23 or 24–79 CE), and the Jewish-Roman historian Josephus (37–100 CE). Philo briefly discusses the Essenes as pious ascetics who lived a communal life, and Pliny says that they lived on the western shore of the Dead Sea (where Qumran sits). Josephus gives the most detailed information, in his works *The Jewish War* and *Jewish Antiquities*.

Josephus discusses three main philosophical schools of religious Jews in the first century CE: Pharisees, Sadducees, and Essenes. He describes their asceticism according to strict rules and discusses the process of admittance to the sect, as well as consequences for not following the community's guidelines. Among these are the sharing of property, renunciation of pleasure, and pursuit of purity, as well as the rejection of marriage and sex. He does note (in an offhand way) that there are two types of Essenes, and one of the groups does not reject marriage but views sex as reserved only for procreation. Josephus also discusses the beliefs of the Essenes, like the immortality of the soul as well as an eschatological belief in punishments and rewards after death as consequences for actions in this life.

Scholars quickly began to associate the Dead Sea Scrolls with the Essenes because of similarities between Josephus's description and the beliefs and practices made apparent in the scrolls. Most important in this regard are documents with guidelines for sectarian communal living, most significantly the *Damascus Document* and the *Community Rule*. In fact, details in these documents fit rather closely with Josephus's account.

Over the years, scholars have disputed whether the Essenes authored the contents of the Dead Sea Scrolls. In many cases, dissenting scholars sought to align the people of Qumran with other early Jewish or proto-Christian sects. Some have pointed out the oddity that none of the scrolls include any explicit reference to the Essenes by name. Professor James VanderKam has pointed out that the authors of some texts in the Scrolls do refer to themselves as "doers of the Torah" and claims that the word for "doers," *ôsê*, is the Semitic root behind the term "Essene" in Greek and Latin sources (VanderKam, "The Dead Sea Scrolls," page 137). Despite some disagreement, most scholars believe that the Essenes were responsible for writing and hiding the Dead Sea Scrolls.

The Community Rule

FACTS

Also known as:	*(Book of the) Rule of the Community, Manual of Discipline, Serekh haYahad,* 1QS
Author:	Unknown member of the Qumran community
Date written:	Between about 100 and 75 BCE
Language:	Hebrew
Canons:	None

DISCOVERY

Before the discovery of the Dead Sea Scrolls, fragments were discovered among the Cairo Geniza documents in 1897. The Dead Sea scroll that contains the *Community Rule* was one of the first scrolls discovered in Cave 1, in 1947. It was among the first publications of the Dead Sea Scrolls, with the first edition appearing in 1951, edited by Millar Burrows. Other fragments were later discovered in Caves 4 and 5.

SUMMARY

Much of what we know about the beliefs and practices of the sectarian Jewish people who lived in or around Qumran comes from the *Community Rule*. It includes an introduction, liturgy of initiation, instruction about the Two Spirits and Two Ways, rules for the community, description of the foundation of the community, and the Master's Hymn.

The first section establishes the *Rule* as a covenant, setting up the sectarian life as an extension of the Covenant in the Torah. It identifies the members of the sectarian community as the "sons of light" and their enemies as the "sons of darkness." A liturgy of initiation follows, outlining a ceremony for those admitted into the community. This concerns what is said and done during the initiation, culminating in baptism.

The text continues with some of the core beliefs of the community. Much of this revolves around belief in "Two Spirits," the "Prince of Light" and the "Angel of Darkness." The "Two Ways" are established as a system of virtues and vices. The *Rule* discusses the consequences of following these Two Ways as rewards or punishments after death. The section concludes with a description of a war between the two forces at the End (*eschaton*), concluding with God's judgment and final purification of all. (See the *War Scroll*, page 60.)

Next follow requirements for adhering to the sectarian life. Here the *Rule* specifies practices that align with Josephus's description, like the process of admittance into the community, common property, and eating meals together. The latter part of this section concerns rules mainly about prohibitions for members of the community. Many of these parallel the Ten Commandments (as in Exodus 20:2–17 and Deuteronomy 5:6–21), while others are more specific. Notable examples include prohibitions against uttering the name of God, insulting a companion, speaking foolishly, being naked before companions or dressing so poorly that public nakedness could accidentally happen, guffawing foolishly or dramatically gesticulating, slandering companions, and murmuring against the community's leaders.

The description of the foundation of the community addresses the organization in a hierarchy, with twelve leaders, three priests, and the Master. It also lays out information about the Council of the Community and their duties. This ends with rules of conduct for the Master, many of which focus on defeating the sons of darkness. Finally, the *Rule* concludes with a Hymn of the Master.

The *Community Rule* is followed on the same scroll by another, shorter set of sectarian guidelines known as the *Rule of the Congregation* (or *Messianic Rule*) and a series of blessings.

ANALYSIS

Significantly, *Community Rule* is parallel to accounts of the Essenes given by Philo and Josephus, but it adds a number of details about the everyday life, rituals, and practices of the sectarian community responsible for the Dead Sea Scrolls. The Covenant is central, as the strict lifestyle is a way of living out holiness for the community as a separate group in a special relationship with God. The *Rule* acts as an extension of the Torah for an exclusive group of elect "chosen ones." It establishes the Essenes as a microcosm of Israelite society with a clear hierarchy of Master, priests, and elders over a group of chosen people who share common ideals.

The *Rule* contains quite a bit of theological content. From the start, the outlook is dualist, emphasizing a split between good (Light) and evil (Darkness), ruled by God and the archdemon Belial. This dualism is evident throughout, especially in the instruction about the Two Spirits. It promotes a deterministic view, concerned with God's foreknowledge of and power over the fate of the two sides in the final battle.

Much of the *Rule* is eschatological in outlook—that is, it is concerned with death, judgment, and the final fate of the soul. Intense regard for the fate of human souls is an extension of the dualist and deterministic system. Some of this represents anxieties about the destiny of the souls of the community, but there are larger cosmic ramifications. The cosmic aspects of the dualistic battle between good and evil, as well as the eschatological consequences, are most pronounced in the description of the final battle and God's judgment. With all of this in mind, the *Rule* presents certain aspects of apocalyptic expectation, related to the apocalyptic literature discussed later in this book, especially in chapter 8.

THE BIBLE AND THE DEAD SEA SCROLLS

Of the manuscripts found among the Dead Sea Scrolls, 223 contain copies of books of the Hebrew Bible. As already mentioned, copies of every book except for Esther and Nehemiah survive, so most of the Hebrew Bible is accounted for. In fact, many biblical books survive in multiple copies. What became obvious to researchers, however, is that these copies of biblical books represent different versions of the Hebrew Bible.

Before the scrolls were discovered, scholars knew of three major versions: the Masoretic Text (the standard basis of most modern translations), the Greek Septuagint, and the Samaritan Pentateuch, which all differ in details.

The Dead Sea Scrolls that contain portions of the Hebrew Bible predate any of the previously known surviving manuscripts of the biblical texts by hundreds of years. This was important for informing much of what modern scholars know about the text of the Hebrew Bible and its status in early Judaism.

Significantly, different copies of biblical books found among the Dead Sea Scrolls correspond to previously known versions of the Hebrew Bible, as well as to other versions with distinct differences. In some cases, the Dead Sea Scrolls confirm the biblical texts known in the later Masoretic Text, but in other cases they are very different. What the Dead Sea Scrolls show us, then, is that even the Hebrew Bible was not fixed in the early Jewish period, and diverse versions existed alongside each other (see Mroczek, *Literary Imagination*). As we will see, this fluidity of the text for the Hebrew Bible is related to the fluidity between biblical and apocryphal literature more generally.

The Great Psalms Scroll

FACTS

Also known as: 11QPsᵃ
Author: Unknown, compiled by a member of the Qumran
                  community; attributed to King David
Date written: Various, compiled between about 30 and 50 CE
Language: Hebrew
Canons: See below

DISCOVERY

This scroll was among the last recovered, from Cave 11, in February 1956. Soon afterward, the Palestine Archaeological Museum in Jerusalem purchased the main portion of the scroll and later other fragments of it. The scroll was initially unrolled in 1961. Because of the time it took to analyze and reconstruct the contents, the text of the Great Psalms Scroll was not published until 1965, edited by James A. Sanders.

SUMMARY

The Great Psalms Scroll is one of the largest of the Dead Sea Scrolls and among the best preserved. It is one of the most significant scrolls for examining interrelations between biblical and apocryphal texts in the collection.

The scroll is damaged at the beginning but probably began with Psalm 101. It contains a variety of biblical and apocryphal psalms, in an order unlike that found in the canonical Hebrew Bible: 101–103, 112, 109–110, 113–118, 104, 147, 105, 146, 148, 120–132, 119, 135–136 & Catena, 145, 154, Plea for Deliverance, 139, 137–138, Sirach 51, Apostrophe to Zion, 93, 141, 133, 144, 155, 142–143, 149-150, Hymn to the Creator, David's Last Words, Account of David's Poems, 140, 134, 151A–B.

A few aspects of this collection of psalms are especially notable. First, although the scroll contains the majority of Psalms 101–150, it does not contain them all. Second, the organization is radically different from the standard order of the Psalter (Book of Psalms) as modern Jews and Christians know it. Finally, the collection includes quite a few apocryphal additions throughout.

Some of the apocryphal psalms (154 and 155) are known from medieval Syriac manuscripts, which sometimes include five extra psalms (151–155). The presence of Sirach 51 is strange, since that is not a psalm but a wisdom poem. Other apocryphal psalms are unique to this scroll. The subjects of most of these are apparent from their titles, and they range in content much like the canonical Psalms.

Particularly notable are apocryphal additions that provide biographical information about David, the purported author of the Psalms. We find the fragment titled "David's Last Words" (containing only a snippet, since the scroll is damaged), immediately followed by a prose account about David as a poet that attributes 4,050 psalms and songs to him. The whole scroll ends with the Hebrew version of Psalm 151, about David, in two parts.

ANALYSIS

The most obvious aspects of the Great Psalms Scroll show that it is idiosyncratic compared to later manuscripts of the Psalter. As Professor Eva Mroczek has shown (in *Literary Imagination*), the scroll defies modern assumptions about the contents and organization of the Psalms and the canonicity of certain parts of the Bible. Psalms 154 and 155 were previously known in Syriac, but scholars now assume they were composed in Hebrew and revered early on. The other apocryphal psalms were also most likely composed in Hebrew, as found in this scroll. In addition to different content and organization, the canonical psalms included in this scroll contain specific textual details divergent from the Masoretic Text and Septuagint.

Like other copies of biblical books found among the Dead Sea Scrolls, this one exhibits the fluidity of biblical and apocryphal texts in the early period. In other words, this collection is *precanonical*, as it demonstrates that the Psalter had not yet taken on the fixed, standard form that later became known as canonical in Jewish and Christian traditions (see Mroczek, *Literary Imagination*).

Some of the apocryphal texts highlight the Davidic nature of the Psalms as a collection. Psalm 151 A–B provide background about David's life, while the "Account of David's Poems" gives information about his poetic abilities, and "David's Last Words" (though fragmentary) adds a final composition for his life. Some scholars have linked this focus on David's life to messianism in the psalms collection, since David is often seen as a typological figure of the awaited Messiah.

Other Psalms scrolls similarly present collections that seem strange to modern readers. For example, a scroll from Cave 4 (4QPs[f]) includes Psalms 22, 107 and 109, the same "Apostrophe to Zion" found in the Great Psalms Scroll, an "Eschatological Hymn," and an "Apostrophe to Judah"; another scroll from Cave 11 (11QPsAp[a], or 11QApocryphal Psalms) includes three psalms for exorcism unknown before the discovery of the Dead Sea Scrolls, and Psalm 91 (also intended for exorcism).

Taken together, these psalms scrolls do underscore the canonicity of the book of Psalms for the sectarian group, but they also show the fluidity of biblical traditions, as well as the canonicity of apocryphal texts alongside them.

The War Scroll

FACTS

Also known as: The War of the Sons of Light against the Sons of Darkness, 1QM

Author: Unknown, possibly a member of the Qumran community

Date written: Between about 150 BCE and 70 CE

Language: Hebrew

Canons: None

DISCOVERY

The *War Scroll* was one of the first scrolls discovered in Cave 1, in 1947. It was among the first publications of the Dead Sea Scrolls, with the first edition appearing in 1954 in Hebrew (1955 in English), edited by Eliezer Sukenik. Unfortunately, it is heavily damaged and posed challenges for analysis and reconstruction of the contents. Other fragments were later discovered in Cave 4 and help fill in some gaps in the text in the main scroll.

SUMMARY

The *War Scroll* is a composite text, compiled from earlier pieces into a single surviving account of the eschatological "War of the Sons of Light with the Sons of Darkness." It is structured into four sections, including an introduction, discussion of organization and tactics, a series of military liturgies, and a description of the future war between Israel and an opposing power referred to as the Kittim.

The introduction establishes the cosmic war between the Israelites and their enemies—the "sons of light" on God's side against the "sons of darkness" on the archdemon Belial's side. The culmination of this long-standing opposition will end in "battle and terrible carnage" in a final apocalyptic war.

Next are enumerated the preparations for war. First is the organization of soldiers, beginning with the High Priest and the priests over the twelve tribes of Israel. The following "rules" for preparation for battle include incantations that the Israelites are supposed to include on the war trumpets and standards. Some of these include epithets such as "The Called of God" and "The Army of God," while others include evocations like "The mighty Deeds of God shall Crush the Enemy, Putting to Flight all those who Hate Righteousness and bringing Shame on those who Hate Him" and "The Wrath of God is Kindled against Belial and against the Men of his Company, Leaving no Remnant." Also in this section appear directions about the weapons, the infantry and cavalry, the ages of the soldiers, the camp, and the duties of the Priests and Levites. Notably, the section about the ages of the soldiers includes an explicit exclusion of children, women, and those "afflicted with a lasting bodily blemish, or smitten with a bodily impurity," like illnesses and disabilities. The section ends with directions to inscribe on the shields and war towers the names of the archangels Michael, Gabriel, Sariel, and Raphael.

Following the preparation for war comes a series of liturgical compositions. Among these are a battle prayer, a victory prayer, a thanksgiving prayer, and a speech by the high priest before the battle against the Kittim.

The end of the *War Scroll* contains an account of the final battle between the Israelites and the Kittim, comprising a series of detailed tactics of the two armies. The whole section is made up of an account of attacks and counterattacks in quick succession, culminating in the victory of the Israelites and God over the Kittim and Belial. Another, final hymn of rejoicing is included before a brief report about the aftermath of the battle.

The conclusion of the account's resolution is cut off. There are also fragments from Caves 4 and 11 called the *Rule of War* (4Q285, 11Q14) that some scholars believe represent the lost ending of the *War Scroll*.

ANALYSIS

Like the *Community Rule* (page 53)—and other Second Temple Jewish works—this document is highly eschatological, relying on a dualist and deterministic system of good and evil. It incorporates sustained apocalyptic imagery and clearly draws on early apocalyptic literature, like Daniel 10–12. This helps to set a date after the composition of Daniel (around 164 BCE). The *War Scroll* consistently establishes a cosmic dualist antagonism between Israel as the "sons of light," who follow God, and their enemies, the "sons of darkness" and the "Kittim," who follow the archdemon Belial. There is a heavy insistence on theology about the Covenant, as the Israelites are those who follow God's Covenant, and their enemies are called "the violators of the covenant." The text further includes divine help in the form of angelic aid from Michael, Gabriel, Sariel, and Raphael. As in other eschatological and apocalyptic works, the outcome of the "time of great tribulation" is God's judgment, resulting in "the battle of destruction of the sons of darkness" and "its end in eternal redemption" for the chosen ones of Israel.

While it does abound in apocalyptic imagery, this work demonstrates a mix of generic characteristics. It is, therefore, representative of a range of types of writing from Second Temple Judaism. In a sense, it is a prophetic text, as it purports to reveal details about the future war. At the same time, some parts are stylized as guidelines for the chosen ones, using the same language of "the rule" found in the *Community Rule*. Large portions are liturgical, including long prayers and hymns for battle, victory, and thanksgiving.

Finally, the whole text is compiled as a war manual, to be read in preparation for the event it describes. It incorporates military logistics, like details about the organization of armies, tactics, weapons, and battle imagery. In all of this, there is a veneration of the priests, who lead and direct the army of the Israelites. At their head is the High Priest. In this text, then, priestly duties are not only religious but also militaristic.

It is not exactly known to whom the Kittim of the scroll refers, although there are some clues. Scholars have pointed out that parts of this text exhibit knowledge of battles and tactics as found in the books of the Maccabees, in which the Jewish people opposed Seleucid forces. Other scholars have studied the military tactics and details and determined that they reflect the practices of Roman legions from the late first century BCE.

Additional Material from the Dead Sea Scrolls

GENESIS APOCRYPHON

This apocryphon was probably composed in Aramaic (as found in Cave 1) sometime between about 200 and 100 BCE, and the scroll found at Qumran is dated approximately between 25 BCE and 50 CE. It relates a paraphrase of parts of Genesis, often from the perspective of the main characters. It is fragmentary, but in its present state it relates the miraculous birth of Noah and then an account of his life in the first person. After the Flood, Noah has a vision about trees, and the text offers an interpretation of the dream in terms of Noah's life as a righteous man. The rest of the narrative concerns Abraham's life, much of it told from his perspective. Some aspects of the text seem related to *Jubilees* (although it is unclear how, exactly), while parts about Enoch and Noah probably rely on *1 Enoch* or common traditions.

BOOK OF NOAH

Although scholars believe that a full *Book of Noah* once existed in Hebrew, pieces survive only in quotations in *Jubilees* and a larger portion used in *1 Enoch*, as well as fragments in Hebrew and Aramaic from Qumran. If all of this fragmentary evidence is from the same lost book, it was likely composed before about 200 BCE. Fragments from Qumran Caves 1 and 6 feature Noah's birth, while fragments from Cave 4 provide a description of the Messiah, discussing physical attributes as well as virtues.

CHAPTER FIVE

Other Gospels

Defining the term "gospel" is tricky business, but doing so is important for understanding a significant genre of Christian apocrypha. The Greek word for "gospel" (*evangelion*) had a range of meanings in the first century CE, including "good news" like imperial proclamations. As early Christianity flourished, the term took on different meanings associated with Jesus's life, death, resurrection, and teachings.

For the most part, gospels come in two types: biographies concerning Jesus's life, crucifixion, resurrection, and post-resurrection ministry; and collections of teachings attributed to Jesus. Many people are familiar with the canonical gospels of Matthew, Mark, Luke, and John, which mainly present biography interspersed with Jesus's teachings. The works in this chapter give a sense of some prominent and representative examples of apocryphal gospels. In some cases, these gospels fill in gaps around Jesus's life that do not appear in the New Testament—like biographies of Jesus's parents, Mary and Joseph; narratives about Jesus's childhood; and what happened to Jesus between his crucifixion and resurrection. In other cases, they provide alternative teachings to those encountered in the canonical gospels. In every case, each gospel presents yet another facet of the diversity of ideas about Jesus across the centuries.

Infancy Gospel of James

FACTS

Also known as: Protevangelium of James, Proto-Gospel of James,
Gospel of Pseudo-James

Author: Unknown, possibly a Jewish Christian; attributed to
James, brother of Jesus

Date written: Between about 150 and 200 CE

Language: Greek

Canons: Not part of any canon, but popular in various
Christian communities, especially in Eastern
Orthodox Christianity

DISCOVERY

Knowledge of this work in Eastern Greek Christianity begins in
the second century and continues to the present. It first appeared
in print in 1552, in a Latin translation by Guillaume Postel, and
in 1564 in a Greek edition by Michael Neander. Scholarly study
did not take off until Johann Albert Fabricius published it in
his collection of apocrypha in 1703. Scholars have continued to
discover manuscripts of other versions, including translations in
Arabic, Armenian, Coptic, Ge'ez, Georgian, Latin, Church Slavic,
and Syriac.

SUMMARY

Although this work is classified as an "infancy gospel," it is more a
biography of Mary than of Jesus. The initial conflict begins when
the righteous man Joachim takes his sacrifice to the temple but is
rejected for his infertility. In despair, he retreats into the desert for
forty days and forty nights. While separated, Joachim and his wife,
Anna, are visited by an angel, who tells them that Anna will conceive. Anna dedicates the child to a life of service to God.

As a baby, Mary is exceptional, as she is able to walk on her own at six months old. At three years old, Anna and Joachim take Mary to the temple, where she spends her childhood in service to God. When she reaches the age of twelve, the priests become concerned about Mary's purity. An angel directs them in a complex process to determine who should be betrothed to Mary, and Joseph is selected.

Mary is visited by an angel and told that she will conceive of the Messiah, to be named Jesus, although she will remain a virgin. Mary visits her pregnant cousin Elizabeth. Joseph discovers Mary's pregnancy and is offended, but an angel sets him right by telling him that she has conceived by the Holy Spirit. When the temple priests learn about Mary's pregnancy, Mary and Joseph stand trial. They are intensely cross-examined and undergo a ritual test that includes drinking bitter water and being sent into the wilderness. They pass the test and are exonerated.

The rest of the narrative concerns the birth and infancy of Jesus. On the way to Bethlehem, Mary experiences a prophetic vision about the division of Jews and Christians, and later Joseph experiences a suspension of time in a vision. Mary gives birth in a cave. A local midwife, Salome, doubts Mary's virginity postpartum, examines her to confirm her virginity, and her hand withers as punishment. After Salome calls out for forgiveness, her hand is restored.

The final chapters generally follow the canonical gospels, with the visit of the Magi and King Herod's wrath about the birth of the Messiah. An episode is added in which Elizabeth and her son, John (the Baptist), hide in a mountain, but her husband, Zechariah, is caught and murdered by Herod's soldiers for not giving up his wife and child.

ANALYSIS

As a biography of Mary's life, the central concern of this gospel is her role in the salvation narrative. The main theme is Mary's purity, as she is consistently portrayed as a model of purity. In fact, the narrative revolves around three major moments that prove Mary's status as a perpetual virgin. The first is during Joseph's questioning her about her pregnancy; the second is the trial by the temple priests; and the third is the midwife's examination after Jesus's birth. By emphasizing Mary's purity, the text offers a sort of explanation about why she was chosen to be the mother of God, and further justification for her veneration as a figure of virginity throughout the rest of her life. Given these themes, and the popularity of this gospel, there must have been an early, intense interest in Mary's life and the theological implications for depictions of her purity.

Gospel of Pseudo-Matthew

FACTS

Also known as: Early versions are titled "Nativity of Saint Mary"; later manuscripts add "and the infancy of our Savior"

Author: Unknown; attributed to the apostle Matthew

Date written: Between about 550 and 700 CE

Language: Latin, translated into many European languages

Canons: Not part of any canon, but popular in Western Europe during the Middle Ages

DISCOVERY

Knowledge of this work in Western Christianity is continuous from its composition to the present. Modern scholars began to pay attention to it only in 1832, when Johann Karl Thilo printed the first full edition. The most important edition, until recently, was Constantin von Tischendorf's, printed in 1853, which included the primary work and additions dating to the later medieval period.

SUMMARY

Chapters 1–13 of the *Gospel of Pseudo-Matthew* comprise an adapted translation of the Greek *Infancy Gospel of James*. Like that gospel, this one tells the story of Mary's conception, birth, childhood, and betrothal to Joseph, followed by the story of Jesus's conception, birth, and parts of his early childhood.

Yet this apocryphon includes major differences and expansions. In the early chapters, shifting perspectives between Mary's parents, Joachim and Anna, as well as expansions of the scenes about them apart from each other, increase dramatic tension. The description of Mary's childhood in the temple is more detailed, representing monastic life according to the *Rule of St. Benedict*. The birth of Jesus and inspection of Mary's virginity is expanded, with a second midwife, in order to emphasize the significance of the event.

Chapters 14–24 depict episodes from Jesus's childhood, some unique. Most of this part of the narrative is about the holy family's flight into Egypt to escape King Herod's plot to kill Jesus. It includes Jesus's miracles as an infant along the way and after they arrive in Egypt. In one episode, Jesus and his family approach a cave to rest in it until a group of dragons emerge, threatening them all until Jesus subdues them and they venerate him. Next, the holy family encounters another group of wild animals who venerate Jesus. In later episodes, Jesus commands a palm tree to bend to allow Mary to eat its fruit, creates a shortcut to reduce a thirty-day journey to one day, and causes the idols of pagan gods to fall down before him in an Egyptian temple. The work ends with a local Egyptian governor venerating Jesus for his powers and declaring him to be God.

ANALYSIS

Much of what was said about the *Infancy Gospel of James* can also be said for this apocryphon, but the *Gospel of Pseudo-Matthew* is unique in many ways. It is, after all, a major work in the development of piety toward the Virgin Mary in Roman Catholic tradition. Throughout the narrative, women are consistently featured—including Anna and her maidservant, Mary and the temple virgins, and the two midwives at Jesus's birth—and there is a concerted effort to think about the role of women in salvation history and the beginnings of Christianity. All of this expands on the important roles of women seen in the canonical gospels, but with more details and humanity given, especially to the figure of Mary. Certain details draw on discussions of female virgin purity in the works of early Christian authors. All of these features situate Mary as a model of virginity and asceticism for Christian women to follow.

Infancy Gospel of Thomas

FACTS

Also known as: Early versions are titled "The Childhood (Deeds) of Jesus"

Author: Unknown; attributed to "Thomas the Israelite," perhaps meant to be the doubting apostle

Date written: Between about 150 and 175 CE; early mentions by Christians appear in the late second century

Language: Greek, but scholars have not discovered a version in its original form, so other early versions are important representatives

Canons: Not part of any canon, but popular in various Christian communities, especially in Eastern Orthodox Christianity

DISCOVERY

Modern scholarship on the work began in 1675, when the historian Peter Lambeck printed a passage from a Greek manuscript in a catalog. Soon afterward, other biblical scholars became interested and began to find other copies and print them. The Catholic theologian Jean-Baptiste Cotelier published the first edition of the Greek text (though from an incomplete manuscript version) in 1698, and

Johann Albert Fabricius printed the same text in his major anthology of Christian apocrypha in 1703. Giovanni Luigi Mingarelli first published the full Greek text in 1764, followed by Johannes Carolus Thilo in 1832. In addition to Greek versions, this gospel survives in translations into Arabic, Ge'ez, Georgian, Irish, Latin, Church Slavic, Syriac, and Ukrainian.

SUMMARY

The *Infancy Gospel of Thomas* relates a number of episodes about Jesus wielding his divine powers as a child. It is not a single coherent narrative but a collection of stories covering some of Jesus's deeds between the ages of five and twelve. Because Jesus often acts in unexpected ways (like killing his playmates in anger), this gospel has been rather controversial from early Christianity to the present.

Episodes include Jesus creating a clay bird and bringing it to life; killing playmates who anger him and resurrecting them when chastised; embarrassing his teachers with greater knowledge than they possess; using his powers to carry water in his clothes after his pitcher breaks; causing a field to yield more harvest than is possible in a single planting season; helping Joseph with carpentry by extending a wooden board when it is cut too short; healing his brother James from the bite of a poisonous viper; and healing other children and adults who are hurt, ill, or die. The gospel ends with a version of the story related in Luke 2:41–51, about twelve-year-old Jesus being left behind in Jerusalem and Mary and Joseph finding him teaching in the temple.

ANALYSIS

This gospel was part of the lively development of ideas about Jesus's life before his public ministry as represented in the canonical gospels. It is, in its own way, both entertaining and theologically complex. While some of Jesus's actions could be interpreted as unnecessarily antagonistic, it also highlights Jesus's human qualities. This aspect of Jesus's identity would have been important to early Christians who were still sorting out their views of Jesus and the significance of his divinity in relation to his human life. In many ways, the work represents how the author (and likely other early Christians) attempted to imagine what life would be like for a young boy with divine powers.

Like other ancient biographies, this one tries to reconcile the protagonist's childhood with heroic greatness in adulthood. And many of the episodes foreshadow events in Jesus's later life, as related in the canonical gospels, with his childhood actions playing out as types of precursors to his mature miracles. Notably, many episodes portray anti-Judaism in their representation of Jewish characters in opposition to Jesus and adherents to legalistic standards of living. Throughout the episodes we find themes of life, death, healing, and resurrection; transformation; teaching in parables; and esoteric knowledge.

The *Infancy Gospel of Thomas* exerted significant influence on later works, as it was widespread in many translations. The story of Jesus bringing a clay bird to life is briefly referred to in the Qur'an. Some portions of the work were translated into Latin and included in manuscripts to expand the *Gospel of Pseudo-Matthew* in the later Middle Ages.

Fragments of Jesus's Teachings

FACTS

Also known as: Agrapha, Logion ("sayings")
Author: Unknown, various
Date written: Various, many in works from about 50–200 CE
Language: Various, many in Greek, Coptic, Latin, and Arabic
Canons: None

DISCOVERY

Scholars have identified hundreds of apocryphal teachings attributed to Jesus from many sources. The "discovery" of these teachings began in the early Christian period and has continued to the present. Many sayings are known from early Christians such as Clement of Rome, Papias of Hierapolis, Justin Martyr, Clement of Alexandria, Origen of Alexandria, and Jerome of Stridon. Others appear scattered throughout other apocrypha, like acts of the apostles. The Qur'an includes a number of Jesus's teachings not recorded elsewhere. Many fragments with such teachings have emerged in finds from the desert, like the Nag Hammadi Codices and Oxyrhynchus Papyri discovered in Egypt.

SUMMARY

Noncanonical teachings attributed to Jesus are often known as "agrapha," meaning "unwritten" (not in the Bible) or "logion" (plural "logia"), meaning "saying." Because there are hundreds of sayings attributed to Jesus found across dozens of writings and many early fragments of papyri, there is no simple summary of them all. It is more helpful to survey some examples.

Many of these teachings are proverbial, like those found in the Beatitudes of Jesus delivered at the Sermon on the Mount or other parts of the canonical gospels. The most popular is the command "Be good money-changers," which is reported in about seventy different early Christian sources. Clement of Rome records a saying much like the biblical "Golden Rule"—do to others as you would have them do to you—which begins, "Be merciful, that you may obtain mercy. Forgive, that you may be forgiven" (*1 Clement* 13:2). Jerome reports another, supposedly from the lost *Gospel of the Hebrews*: "And only then shall you be glad, when you look on your brother with love" (*Commentary on Ephesians* 5:4). Origen claims, "I have read somewhere as a word of the Savior . . ." and records the saying "The one who is close to me is close to the fire. The one who is far from me is far from the kingdom" (*Homilies on Jeremiah* 3.3). Similar to the wise man who built his house upon a rock (Matthew 7:24–27), the seventh teaching in the Oxyrhynchus Logia reports Jesus saying, "A city built upon the top of a hill and established can neither fall nor be hid."

Other teachings are more like parables. For instance, Papias reports one that supposedly came from the apostle John, in which Jesus states, "The days will come, in which vines shall grow, each having ten thousand branches, and in each branch ten thousand twigs, and in each true twig ten thousand shoots . . ." (recorded in Irenaeus's *Against Heresies* 5.33.3), continuing on with a point about a hope for a future paradise, not unlike such expectations in the gospels and other apocalyptic works.

ANALYSIS

Noncanonical teachings of Jesus are both similar to teachings found in the canonical gospels and diverse in content. They demonstrate a range of form (from long to short), generic characteristics (like proverbs and parables), and difficulty of ideas (from simple to challenging to interpret).

One major scholarly question is if these sayings come from lost gospels. A related question is whether or not these fragments represent Jesus's "authentic" teachings. No definitive answers to either question are likely to emerge. Like many other apocrypha, perhaps the key is not in sources or authenticity but in understanding these sayings as snapshots of what some Christians have believed about Jesus's teachings, and to consider why those beliefs matter for the long history of Christianity.

Gospel of Thomas

FACTS

Author: Unknown, probably a Syrian Christian; attributed to the apostle Didymus ("Twin") Judas Thomas, supposedly (according to Syriac Christians especially) Jesus's twin brother

Date written: Compiled between about 100 and 120 CE, with some of the oldest portions possibly from between about 30 and 60 CE

Language:	Greek, but only fragments survive; the full text is preserved in a Coptic book from Nag Hammadi, translated no later than the middle of the fourth century
Canons:	None

DISCOVERY

For most of the history of Christianity, the so-called *Gospel of Thomas* was known only from testimonies by early Christian writers, mainly condemnations. Greek fragments were discovered in a stash of papyrus documents at Oxyrhynchus in Egypt by Bernard Pyne Grenfell and Arthur Surridge Hunt in 1897 and 1903. When the Nag Hammadi Codices were discovered in Egypt in 1945, a full version of the text in Coptic was among them, and scholars were able to identify it as the source for the previously found sayings. This gospel is the most popular and most studied of the Nag Hammadi texts.

SUMMARY

Unlike many gospels, the *Gospel of Thomas* does not have a narrative about Jesus's life; instead, it is a collection of independent sayings compiled together. The standard numbering runs to 114 sayings, but since some numbered sections contain multiple sayings, there are many more. It begins simply: "These are the hidden sayings that the living Jesus spoke and Didymus Judas Thomas recorded" (1). The sayings range in form and content, including proverbs, parables, commands, dialogue with his followers, and more. Because there are so many, it is not possible to summarize them all, but there are some notable examples.

Many sayings are parallel to the canonical gospels. Some concern "the kingdom of heaven" (20, 8, and 34), comparable to teachings in Mark 4:30–32, Matthew 13:47–50, and Luke 6:39/Matthew 15:14. In saying 16, Jesus talks about bringing conflict into the world, with parallels to Matthew 10:34–36 and Luke 12:51–53.

These are just a few examples of the types of parallels with the synoptic gospels.

A handful of sayings are unique to *Thomas*, and some are more mysterious than others. One states, "Blessed is the lion that the human will eat, so that the lion becomes human. And cursed is the human that the lion will eat, and the lion will become human" (7). Another says, "Do not worry, from morning to evening and from evening to morning, about what you will wear" (36). Saying 42 states, simply and enigmatically, "Be passersby," or (in another translation) "Become transients." Saying 112 offers a comment on spiritual dualism: "Woe to the flesh that depends on the soul. Woe to the soul that depends on the flesh." Other sayings are longer conversations or parables. Saying 97 likens the Father's kingdom to a jar that breaks while a woman carries it home and spills out its contents along the way. Immediately following, the enigmatic saying 98 compares the Father's kingdom to the murder of a powerful person.

Finally, the gospel ends with a puzzling saying about turning Mary (presumably Mary Magdalene) into a male, as Jesus says, "For every female who makes herself male will enter heaven's kingdom" (114).

ANALYSIS

As a collection of sayings, the form of this gospel is akin to wisdom writings from the Hebrew Bible and Second Temple Judaism, like Proverbs, Ecclesiastes, *Wisdom of Ben Sira*, and *Wisdom of Solomon*. It also shows the development of wisdom literature toward rabbinic literature in the first centuries of the Common Era, and the types of teachings incorporated in early Christian gospels.

Despite lacking a biographical frame about Jesus's life, this gospel is intimately connected to the synoptic gospels of Matthew, Mark, and Luke. It shares many parallels with these canonical gospels. In fact, some scholars believe that parts of *Thomas* are based on or perhaps represent a lost source (called "Q," from the German word for source, *Quelle*) for sayings used across the gospels. This "Q source" was likely an early collection of Jesus's teachings, much like *Thomas*, which was used by the authors of the canonical Gospels of Matthew and Luke. Following this reasoning, the compiler of *Thomas* likely used the same source or a common source. Some scholars believe that this gospel represents earlier versions of Jesus's teachings than the canonical parallels. At the same time, some scholars believe that sayings in *Thomas* (or parts of it) have been influenced by the synoptic gospels.

Although it was found among works at Nag Hammadi that have been categorized as "Gnostic," this gospel is not considered to be composed by Gnostic Christians. Nonetheless, this gospel is a significant witness to alternative early Christian views of Jesus. Some scholars have argued that the Gospel of John poses a response to the *Gospel of Thomas*, amounting to evidence of conflict among early Christians. From that perspective, *John* represents the theological view that became orthodox, while *Thomas* represents a view that was deemed "heretical" by the winners in this conflict. This gospel is notable for its many enigmatic sayings, which need to be interpreted—some leading to a certain amount of scholarly debate. All of this casts Jesus as a wisdom figure, dispensing knowledge that is otherwise unknown or unattainable. At the same time, many of the enigmatic sayings in this collection are not all that different from the canonical gospels, which represent Jesus as a teacher with often unconventional wisdom.

Gospel of Nicodemus

FACTS

Also known as: Acts of Pilate, Descent into Hell
Author: Unknown; attributed to Nicodemus, from the Gospel of John
Date written: Earliest core in the third century, later parts composed by the sixth or seventh century, all compiled together by the ninth century

Language:	Greek and Latin, translated into dozens of other European and Near Eastern languages
Canons:	Not part of any canon, but the Latin version was wildly popular in Western Europe

DISCOVERY

Knowledge of this work has been unbroken from its composition to the present. It was so popular that it was among the first printed books in Europe, with at least four printings before 1500, five more in the sixteenth century, and many more afterward. Johann Albert Fabricius published it in his collection of apocrypha in 1703, and Constantin von Tischendorf published it in his collection in 1853. Although flawed, Tischendorf's remain the standard editions of the Greek and Latin texts.

SUMMARY

The earliest core of the *Gospel of Nicodemus* comprises chapters 1–11, the *Acts of Pilate*, concerning Jesus's trial, crucifixion, resurrection, and ascension; later were added chapters 12–16, about Joseph of Arimathea; and then chapters 17–27, the *Descent into Hell*, relating Jesus's journey to hell after his crucifixion to free the righteous from captivity.

The first part is a lively account of the Roman trial of Christ before Pontius Pilate, incorporating pieces from the canonical gospels as well as additional details. One moment in the trial, for instance, deals with Jesus's parentage and witnesses to Joseph and Mary's marriage. Nicodemus appears on Jesus's behalf and attests to his miracles. Next appear several witnesses who have been healed by Jesus's miracles. Eventually, the Jewish leaders and the crowd demand Jesus's death, and the narrative retells his crucifixion.

In the second part, because Joseph of Arimathea asks to bury Jesus's body, he is arrested as a sympathizer and kept in jail until after the sabbath. Afterward, soldiers report Jesus's disappearance to Pilate, and Joseph reports how Jesus appeared to him at midnight. A series of other witnesses are brought forth to confirm Jesus's resurrection and ascension, and these testimonies convince the Jewish leaders and all the people to believe.

The third part features two sons of Simeon (from Luke 2:28–35) who have recently died but were resurrected. They are asked what they saw while dead and write two identical accounts of Jesus's Harrowing of Hell. This includes a number of conversations, like those between Adam and his son Seth and between Satan and Hades. The climax of the narrative depicts Jesus busting down the gates of hell with a band of angels, binding Satan in chains, and rescuing the Jewish patriarchs, prophets, martyrs, and saints—taking them all to heaven. The accounts written by the two men are sealed up and the men disappear.

Several other texts (about Pilate and related subjects) were often added to this gospel in medieval manuscripts, creating a complex set of relationships between them.

ANALYSIS

The main story is meant as a series of narratives and eyewitness accounts about Jesus's miracles and resurrection in order to convert skeptical Roman leaders within the story. At the same time, this gospel's insistence on such eyewitness testimonies works like a series of authenticating stories to corroborate the canonical gospels and expand them with further details. The story of the Harrowing works not only as a witness to Jesus's actions before resurrection but also as an answer to the question of where the righteous patriarchs of the Hebrew Bible will spend eternity.

The *Descent into Hell* was especially influential on Roman Catholic doctrine about the Harrowing of Hell and even appeared in medieval liturgical texts for worship in Easter services. Scenes of the Harrowing continue to pervade art and popular ideas about Jesus's actions between his crucifixion and resurrection. No doubt this popularity was due to the way this gospel provides compelling details about what happened to Jesus between his crucifixion and resurrection, which were not explored in the canonical gospels.

CHAPTER SIX

Gnostic Texts

A s early Christianity developed, prominent authoritative voices condemned certain texts and people as heretical because they were *gnostikos* (in Greek), or Gnostic. Eventually, those authorities won out as the voices of orthodoxy. Over the centuries, a range of evidence has been recovered to shed light on the early Christian movement often called "gnosticism." Still, much remains a mystery.

In 1945, near the Egyptian town of Nag Hammadi, a set of thirteen Coptic codices (books) were found. The Nag Hammadi Codices (NHC) were copied in the third and fourth centuries, but they generally represent older texts. Most of these texts were previously known only in references by early Christians, and they contain ideas that have helped scholars to redefine and better understand early Christianities.

In short, those Christians who are now called "Gnostics" believed in a theology rooted in seeking secret knowledge (*gnosis*) as the key to salvation and liberation from the material world. Such gnosis includes knowledge attained from both mystical unity with the divine and understanding oneself within the cosmos. Gnostic philosophy derives much from Neoplatonism, like dualist ideas about the material world and immaterial reality. The texts demonstrate a synthesis of philosophical concepts in early Christianity, which drew on not only Jewish thought but also ideas from Greek, Egyptian, and other Near Eastern cultures. This was especially true in Hellenistic Egypt, where Jews had lived in diaspora for hundreds of years, and where Christianity took hold early in the spread of this new religion. The resulting teachings, as seen in the NHC, were a sort of mash-up of biblical teachings with metaphysical concerns from other cultures.

According to Gnostic ideas, the world (material and immaterial) was created by the Demiurge (Yahweh, the God of the Hebrew Bible, often called Yaldabaoth), but humans were imprisoned in the earthly, physical realm of existence. All of this gives rise to a rejection of this world's materiality in order to achieve liberated existence into eternal transcendence. Jesus Christ was sent by a higher, unknowable divine Light, in order to offer liberation through gnosis. The goal of Gnostic scriptures is to help believers on the path to spiritual transcendence and reunification with the true God.

This overview might give a general sense, but these are generalizations. Recently, scholars have found that the concept of Gnosticism encompasses a range of ideas held by diverse groups rather than a single coherent belief system. Some scholars have even called for abandoning the terms "gnostic" and "gnosticism" because they are too generalizing or anachronistic to be useful in discussing specific texts. In many cases, scholars prefer to discuss "Gnostic" texts as representatives of more precise categories—like Sethian or Valentinian Christianities. Certain characteristics of these two types of thought become clearer by looking at specific works among the NHC and related texts.

One small thing to note in this chapter is that the NHC texts are designated according to their codex (book) and the text number within that book; some texts are designated according to other manuscripts they survive in.

Gospel of Truth

FACTS

Witness: NHC Codex I, 3 and Codex XII, 2
Author: Unknown; possibly composed by the Christian
theologian Valentinus
Date written: Between about 140 and 180 CE
Language: Originally Greek, but survives only in Coptic
(one full version and one fragment)
Canons: None

SUMMARY

While the *Gospel of Truth* is titled a "gospel," in form and function
it is more like a homily or sermon. It provides an exposition that
interprets "the gospel," or "good news" of salvation brought about
by Jesus Christ, the Savior, with the central victory as the Savior's
defeat of Error. This is established at the start, which explains that
Error entered the cosmos and "grew powerful" in her use of "material substance" and "forgetfulness" to deceive the Father's creation.
The gospel explains Jesus's role in bringing the Father's knowledge
to the world so that people can resist Error.

The structure of this gospel is not linear but follows a series of
thematic images. Several derive from the canonical gospels and
are used to reflect on the cosmic significance of Jesus's life, death,
and resurrection. For example, the Parable of the Sheep (Matthew
18:12–14, Luke 15:4–7, *Gospel of Thomas* 107) is evoked to interpret
the gospel story on a cosmic level.

In another complex intertwining of themes from the canonical gospels, emphasis is laid on imagery of Jesus as the Word, the
Father's book of salvation, and metaphors of language, like the
"vowels" and "letters" of the book that signify "truth" and the
Father's eternal knowledge. Jesus's crucifixion is depicted with the
imagery that he "published the Father's edict [about salvation] on
the cross." This thematic imagery of the Word is closely related

to a running thread about names. Part of the gospel discusses the Father uttering the names of his followers and how they call on him, and this is evoked later as the Father's Name is revealed in the Son and his knowledge.

The gospel concludes with a reflection on eschatology (that is, matters concerned with death, judgment, and the final fate of the soul), especially emphasizing a soul's final, cosmic return to "the place of rest" in the "Fullness" (Pleroma) of the Father. The final words offer a poetic affirmation of the Father's love: "For he is good, and his children are perfect and worthy of his Name. Children like this the Father loves."

ANALYSIS

This work has been identified as representative of Valentinian Christianity, associated with the Christian theologian Valentinus (ca. 100–160 CE). As an Egyptian scholar who received a Greek education in Alexandria (a metropolitan center of Hellenistic culture), Valentinus was among the early Christians who attempted to align Christianity with the philosophy of Neoplatonism (from Greek philosophy). The gospel exhibits some major hallmarks of Neoplatonic writings. First is a cosmological conception of a single Monad (supreme divine being, the Father) at the start of the cosmos who emanates a Pleroma ("Fullness") of spiritual beings like the Word (Jesus, the Savior), Truth, and the Holy Spirit, as well as a flawed being (here Error, but often Sophia), who causes disunity and creates the lesser material world. Salvation means reunification with the Pleroma of the Father. Second is the strong identity of a church community (Christians), referred to here as "members of the eternal realm" and in metaphors about the Father's children—the audience of the gospel's exhortations to certain practices. Finally, there are substantial parallels with and allusions to New Testament scriptures, manifested as references to "the gospel" and specific teachings of Jesus like the Parable of the Sheep.

In some respects, this apocryphon is similar to the letters of Paul. Strikingly, the basic theology underlying this work is rather close to what many modern Christians believe to be orthodox. Given how accessible it is, some scholars believe that this text was meant to be preached as a way to welcome outsiders into the author's community of Christians. Some even go so far as to attribute this gospel to Valentinus himself.

Secret Book of John

FACTS

Witnesses:	NHC Codex II, 1; Codex III, 1; Codex IV, 1; and Berlin Gnostic Codex 8502, 2
Also known as:	*Apocryphon of John*
Author:	Unknown; attributed to the apostle John, son of Zebedee
Date written:	Between about 120 and 180 CE
Language:	Originally Greek, but survives only in Coptic
Canons:	None, although a group known as Audian Christians (in Syria and Scythia) used this text at least into the eighth century

DISCOVERY

Unlike most other works in the Nag Hammadi Codices, the *Secret Book of John* is known in four different versions. One was discovered in 1896 in a Coptic book now called the Berlin Gnostic Codex 8502. This codex had been found at a Christian burial site in Akhmim, Egypt, and then bought and taken to the Berliner Museum by Carl Reinhardt. But the texts in the Berlin Gnostic Codex were not published until 1955, by Walter C. Till. In the meantime, the NHC had been found, containing three other versions of the same work.

SUMMARY

The *Secret Book of John* begins with the title figure, who goes to a wilderness mountain to pray in a moment of doubt and experiences an encounter with God the Father, the Mother, and the Child, who offer an explanation of the mysteries of the cosmos. What follows is a rewriting of the creation of the cosmos and humans from the beginning of Genesis.

The first sections are concerned with the order of the cosmos. This begins with the Father, who emanates the Mother, Barbelo; together they conceive the Child, or the Son and Savior. This triune godhead creates a series of aeons, or spiritual beings within the Fullness of the Father, including Pigeradamas (Adam) and his son Seth.

The next section relates the story of the aeon Sophia, the feminine figure of Wisdom, who conceives on her own and creates a monstrous child with "the figure of a snake and the face of a lion" and "eyes like flashing bolts of lightning." This child is the evil Yaldabaoth, who creates his own order of 365 lesser aeons of "angels," establishes the material world, and declares, "I am God and there is no other god beside me." Sophia sees the consequences of her actions, repents, and is reunited with the Fullness.

The rest of the work is taken up with the story of the Father-Mother and Son conspiring against Yaldabaoth in his creation of humans to establish a plot for salvation. Although humans remain imprisoned in the material world, the Father-Mother infuse Adam and Eve and prepare a way for salvation. Meanwhile, the Son induces Adam and Eve to eat of the fruit of the tree of knowledge of good and evil, and gives them a form of gnosis. Yaldabaoth defiles Eve and creates Cain and Abel (also called Elohim and Yahweh), but Adam and Eve conceive Seth, a sort of savior figure.

What follows is a dialogue between John and the Son (the speaker) about human destiny and salvation. The Son reveals that after death, the soul leaves the body and eventually "awakens from forgetfulness and acquires knowledge," leading to salvation and reunification with God's Fullness (Pleroma). All of this is meant to unravel the evil of Yaldabaoth and bring humans into full knowledge of the true God.

The longer version of this work, found in two of the NHC, concludes with a Hymn of the Savior, about Jesus (the Savior) as Forethought, the offspring of the Father-Mother, who offers salvation through gnosis, calls for followers to awaken from their sleep, and evokes the baptismal Rite of the Five Seals.

ANALYSIS

This text contains an exposition of the "Sethian myth" at the core of Sethian Christianity, which prioritized Seth (a son of Adam and Eve) as a spiritual ancestor and savior. Many of the texts attributed to Sethian Christianity (from the second and third centuries CE) display a fusion of Jewish ideas about Seth with Hellenistic philosophy, and some scholars have linked it to similar ideas in Mandeanism and Manicheanism. One of the major elements of this type of Christianity was a preoccupation with Seth, his offspring, and his identity as a savior figure—often in Christological terms—because of his role in giving humans gnosis. Some of the hallmarks of Sethian Christianity are seen in the cosmological order, the story of Sophia (inspired by Hellenistic philosophy), and the salvation myth through Adam and his son Seth, culminating in an esoteric ritual referred to as the baptism of the Five Seals.

In many ways this work is an interpretive retelling of the first several chapters of Genesis through the lens of Sethian mythology. This is signaled by the work's explicit use of quotations from the Hebrew Bible and commentary, as when John is told, "Do not suppose that it is as Moses said . . ." and "It is not as Moses wrote and you heard." In other words, the story in the Hebrew Bible is not to be trusted. Instead, this work establishes its own mythical framework as an explanation for the world and the need for salvation through the Son. Because this work focuses on retelling aspects of the Hebrew Bible, some scholars have suggested that it might pose evidence for early Jewish gnosticism that was later adopted by certain Christians.

Gospel of Philip

FACTS

Witness:	NHC II, 3
Author:	Unknown; attributed to Philip, possibly meant to be the apostle
Date written:	Between about 150 and 250 CE
Language:	Originally Greek, but survives only in Coptic
Canons:	None

SUMMARY

This gospel is another text found among the Nag Hammadi Codices in Egypt. Like the *Gospel of Thomas* (page 73), it does not have the biographical form or function of other gospels, as it is a collection of teachings, numbered 127 in all. The title indicates something more like "the good news" through esoteric teachings, including proverbs, parables, commands, dialogue, and extended reflections. Because there are so many, it is not possible to summarize them all, but there are some notable examples.

Some teachings are distinctly esoteric. For example, "Blessed is one who is before coming into being. For whoever is, was and will be." (64.9–12)

Many teachings concern Jesus's life. Probably the most famous, because it has sparked some sensational theories, is about Jesus and Mary Magdalene: "The companion of the [Savior] is Mary of Magdala. The [Savior loved] her more than [all] the disciples, [and he] kissed her often on her [mouth]." (63.30ff.) Mary Magdalene features elsewhere, too, as in a brief passage about the three women named Mary, identified as Jesus's mother, sister, and companion (Magdalene) (59.6–11). One section concerns Joseph the carpenter planting a garden that sprouted the tree for the cross used to crucify Jesus (73.8–19). Another states that "Jesus tricked everyone, for he did not appear as he was, but he appeared so that he could be seen," and goes on to clarify this claim (57.28–58.10).

Other parts are concerned with reinterpreting the Hebrew Bible. One teaching begins, "God is a man-eater, and so humans are sacrificed to him," and explains that he was not a true god (62.35–63.4). One explains the typological connection between Adam and Christ (71.3–15), while another interprets Abraham's circumcision with a comment on dualism between material and immaterial reality, concluding that he showed that "it is necessary to destroy the flesh" (82.26–29).

Several sayings deal with nakedness. One states, "No one can meet the king while naked" (58.15–17); even though not much earlier there is a section rife with sarcasm that deals with nakedness as a sign of corporeality (56.26–57.22).

Some teachings are eschatological, such as a brief vision of hell by "an apostolic person [who] saw people who were locked up in a house of fire, bound with [chains] of fire, and thrown [into] . . . fire" (66.29–67.1).

Quite a few deal with sacraments, summed up as "The master [did] everything in a mystery: baptism, chrism, eucharist, redemption, and bridal chamber" (67.27–30). Highly metaphorical imagery about marriage and the bridal chamber especially pervades the gospel.

ANALYSIS

As already noted, this gospel is not unlike the *Gospel of Thomas*, although it contains more clearly Gnostic beliefs and diverges from Jesus's teachings in the canonical gospels in striking ways. While some of the contents are attributed to Jesus ("the master"), many are not, and some concern him rather than being attributed to him. Some scholars believe that it was meant as a manual of material for preachers.

Certain aspects of this anthology exhibit characteristics of Valentinian Christianity. The author makes use of the canonical gospels of Matthew and John, as well as 1 Corinthians, which were used in other Valentinian works. Additionally, some specific terms and ways of talking about concepts are characteristic of Valentinian ideas: "perfect light," male-female binaries (or *syzygies*), and emphasis on certain sacraments. Some Valentinian Christians also adhered to a fivefold system of sacraments ("mysteries") as found in this work.

Gospel of Mary

FACTS

Witnesses:	Berlin Gnostic Codex 8502, 1; Papyrus Oxyrhynchus 3525; and Papyrus Rylands 463
Author:	Unknown; attributed to a woman named Mary, probably meant to be Mary Magdalene
Date written:	Between about 100 and 200 CE
Language:	Originally Greek, but only fragments survive; it survives more fully in Coptic
Canons:	None

DISCOVERY

The *Gospel of Mary* was first discovered in 1896 in Akhmim, Egypt, in the pages of what became known as the Berlin Gnostic Codex 8502. Yet the text was not published until 1955, by Walter C. Till. Fragments of the text in Greek were discovered in Papyrus Oxyrhynchus 3525 and Papyrus Rylands 463 by Bernard Pyne Grenfell and Arthur Surridge Hunt between 1807 and 1906, but they were not published until 1983, by P. J. Parsons. None of these witnesses include the full text.

SUMMARY

This apocryphon is a type of gospel known as a post-resurrection dialogue, which reveals Jesus's teachings after his resurrection. Unfortunately, the fullest version of this work is not complete, so it both lacks a beginning and has a large missing portion later in the text.

The gospel begins in the middle of Jesus teaching the disciples about physical matter (like bodies) and the evils of the material world. Jesus tells them, "There is no such thing as sin." The text uses that idea as a basis for contradicting assumptions about the material world, especially by posing the idea that humans do not know better because they lack secret knowledge (gnosis). After commanding the disciples to preach his good news to the world, Jesus departs.

The disciples mourn, but Mary comforts them by offering to tell them Jesus's secret teachings, which he told her in private. She begins by explaining that she had a vision of the Lord (Jesus), in which he instructed her about the mind and its fate. But the text in the Berlin Gnostic Codex breaks off. It picks up again as Mary describes the final step in the ascent of the soul. She explains that the soul was bound by the evil of the material world, but escaped after death. In the end, the soul achieves rest in transcendence.

After her revelation, Mary stands silent in imitation of the soul at rest. The disciples, however, have a problem with Mary's vision. Andrew and Peter challenge her. Peter especially complains about Jesus choosing Mary over the rest as the bearer of his secret knowledge. Levi (the apostle Matthew) speaks up in defense of Mary, although there is no resolution. Instead, the disciples disperse to teach and to preach—but without resolution about the gospel that Mary shared.

ANALYSIS

Unfortunately, because the *Gospel of Mary* is fragmentary, many mysteries remain about its contents. Nonetheless, it is significant for what it tells us about the beliefs of the Christians who wrote and preserved it. The gospel exhibits characteristics of "Gnostic" thought in its reverence for a female authority, focus on the evil of the material world, and description of the soul's ascent. The last aspect especially may be compared to ideas at the end of the *Secret Book of John* (page 83).

This work is the only early Christian gospel attributed to a woman in title, although it is more properly *about* her. In fact, the basic premise of the work emphasizes that Mary is Jesus's most trusted apostle and the one to whom he gave the authority of his true teachings about gnosis for the soul. The ending of the work highlights the trouble with being a woman leader in a patriarchal religion, but it reinforces Mary's role as the most-loved apostle and an authority for some early Christians.

Gospel of Judas

FACTS

Witness:	Codex Tchacos, 3
Author:	Unknown; attributed to the disciple Judas
Date written:	Between about 140 and 180 CE
Language:	Originally Greek, but survives only in Coptic
Canons:	None

DISCOVERY

The modern discovery and publication of the *Gospel of Judas* begins around 1978, when the Coptic codex containing it was discovered near El Minya, Egypt. Over the following decades, it passed through the hands of several antiquities dealers, who treated it poorly. One stuck it in a freezer to preserve it—to opposite effects. Frieda Nussberger-Tchacos (who named it the Codex Tchacos) purchased it in 2000. Finally, in 2006, the Maecenas Foundation for Ancient Art, in Basel, purchased it. The National Geographic Society made the gospel known to the world in 2006, publishing a translation by Rudolphe Kasser, Marvin Meyer, and Gregor Wurst.

SUMMARY

This is a gospel *about* Judas Iscariot, rather than attributed to him. The beginning states that it is "The secret revelatory discourse that

Jesus spoke with Judas." Although there is a narrative to frame Jesus's teachings, most of the work is dialogue.

Jesus comes across the disciples sharing a meal with each other (the Eucharist), and he questions how they know him. The disciples become angry and Judas alone dares to stand before Jesus and declare that he comes from "the immortal realm of Barbelo."

From that point on, Jesus pulls Judas aside for a series of secret teachings. Much of the work includes Jesus's teachings and his interpretations of visions, revealing Judas's fate and the duplicitousness of the other disciples.

A centerpiece of this gospel concerns Jesus's explanation of the order of the cosmos. This section lays out a hierarchy of spiritual beings, including the highest divine being, the Father, the Autogenes, Adamas, the Four Luminaries, and the evil god Yaldabaoth. This section then relates the creation of Adam and Eve, as well as an outline of God's divine plan to grant Adam gnosis that will lead to human salvation.

In Jesus's last teaching, he tells Judas that he will exceed all of the other disciples. He also cryptically reveals that Judas will hand Jesus over as a sacrifice. As Jesus explains, this will lead to human salvation through transcendence to the eternal realms. The work ends with Judas handing Jesus over to the high priests and taking his payment.

ANALYSIS

One of the keys to understanding the *Gospel of Judas* is how one interprets the figure of Judas within the text. Some view him as a hero for the ideal of salvation through gnosis; others view him as a villain; still others see him as a figure carrying out his fate for the salvation of humans. But the text itself is frustratingly ambiguous.

It is clear, however, that this gospel is particularly antagonistic toward certain Christians and rituals. The disciples, besides Judas, are frequently derided and portrayed as opposed to Jesus. At the beginning, the Eucharist is rejected when Jesus laughs at the disciples for the practice. In one of the visions that Jesus interprets, the disciples are portrayed as committing human sacrifice against those they lead astray. This gospel, then, sets up a radical alternative vision of Christianity in the early centuries of the faith.

Although this work exhibits many components typical of "Sethian" Christianity, it lacks a focus on Seth himself, so scholars debate whether it is actually a Sethian gospel. The cosmology especially may be compared to the one in the *Secret Book of John* (page 83). Most likely all of this demonstrates diversity of ideas among Sethian Christians, even though it is often identified as a single community.

Additional "Gnostic" Material

Dozens of other texts categorized as "Gnostic" were found in the Nag Hammadi Codices in Egypt. A few notable examples deserve mention. All of these were likely composed in the second or early third century.

PRAYER OF THE APOSTLE PAUL (NHC I, 1)

This brief prayer is found on the front flyleaf (blank page) of the first of the NHC, probably an addition after the codex had been compiled. The first part presents metaphorical invocations of the Redeemer as mind, treasury, fullness, and rest. The second, longer part includes supplications with imagery reminiscent of canonical biblical texts (the Psalms and Pauline epistles) and "Gnostic" works, as the author asks for gifts, authority, healing of the body, redemption of soul and spirit, knowledge, and the mystery of God's house. It ends with the title and the words "In peace | Holy is Christ" written in Greek. The prayer demonstrates a synthesis between imagery from the Hebrew Bible and Neoplatonic philosophy—even to the point that it uses the Greek philosophical words *nous* (mind), *pleroma* (fullness), and *anapausis* (repose). Some scholars have claimed that it represents Valentinian Christianity.

APOCALYPSE OF ADAM (NHC V, 5)

This work presents a revelation ("apocalypse") of Adam to his son Seth. It retells Genesis from the beginning through stories about Noah's sons Shem, Ham, and Japheth, containing Sethian cosmological lore. Then follows a lengthy hymn about the Illuminator (a savior figure) by Thirteen Kingdoms (called archons). Next follows a section about the salvation of humanity through baptism. It ends with angels preserving the revelation on a "rock of truth" atop an unnamed mountain. It is possible that this work represents an early Jewish form of gnosticism later taken over by Christians.

THUNDER: PERFECT MIND (NHC VI, 2)

One of the more enigmatic works in the NHC, *Thunder* is a discourse written from the first-person perspective of a divine female Wisdom figure who describes herself in contradictions. While the genre is unusual among the NHC, it is like other pieces of ancient wisdom literature in some respects. The speaker is oppressed and speaks of violence toward her; yet she calls for the audience to accept her, seek her, and draw near to her, as she promises eternal life.

CHAPTER SEVEN

Apostolic Texts

There are myriad apocrypha that concern the apostles, have been attributed to the apostles, or are considered products of the "apostolic age" of Christianity. The number of apocrypha under this umbrella grows even more when we include all of the early followers of Jesus not traditionally considered apostles (like Mary Magdalene, Thecla, and so on). This chapter deals with several representative examples of apocrypha related to the apostles in some way.

These works encompass a variety of genres of apocrypha, like acts, letters, and theological treatises. Even within these general categories, there is quite a lot of diversity in literary types. What all of these works have in common is that they came to represent Christian attitudes about Jesus's apostles as early preachers of the gospel and authorities of early Christianity. These works both draw on ideas about apostolic authority and help perpetuate views of the apostles as authoritative figures.

Some of the works discussed here (the *Didache* and *Letter of Barnabas*) are in the category called "Apostolic Fathers" and not often considered alongside apocrypha. Many early Christian theologians considered them to have scriptural authority like the canonical works, even though they later were rejected ecumenically, so their relationship to apocrypha deserves attention.

Despite the question of canonical status for the works discussed in this chapter, most of them have been influential at some point in the history of Christianity. The *Didache* and *Letter of Barnabas* were popular among several early Christian theologians. Many of the acts of apostles were widely circulated and read, and they inspired many works of art during the Middle Ages. In fact, some of these acts still form the basis for Roman Catholic and Eastern Orthodox veneration of the apostles and feasts celebrated annually in commemoration of their lives.

ACTS OF APOSTLES

The earliest account about the apostles' lives after Jesus's ascension was probably the biblical book of the Acts of the Apostles, attributed to Luke, who wrote the canonical gospel associated with his name, around 80–90 CE. Many other narratives about the apostles also proliferated in early Christianity.

Some of the oldest and most influential of these works concern five of the apostles: Andrew, John, Paul, Peter, and Thomas. All of these were composed in the second or third century and were well regarded by Christian communities from that time onward. These five acts recount the missionary activities of the apostles and the circumstances of their deaths. These early acts are quite important and clearly influenced a number of later authors, as they became models for the genre of acts and, later, saints' lives (known as "hagiography").

One of the major aspects of the apocryphal acts is the assignment of the apostles to different regions of the ancient world. For example, each of the apostles in the five early acts traveled to a different location: Andrew to Greece; John to Asia (especially Ephesus); Peter and Paul to the Mediterranean region and Rome; and Thomas to India. Various traditions developed about the associations of these and the other apostles with specific geographies, especially based on local veneration of particular apostles in particular places.

Many of the traditions about where the apostles traveled relate to ideas about the apostles' deaths and burial locations in the apocryphal acts. In the *Acts of Paul*, *Acts of Peter*, and *Martyrdom of Peter and Paul* (a combined narrative), both apostles are martyred in Rome, where their tombs are traditionally located. In the *Acts of John*, he is not martyred, but dies peacefully of old age in Ephesus; some manuscripts relate that his body is taken up (assumed) into heaven after his death.

In addition to early traditions about the apostles' missionary activities and deaths, many apocryphal acts contain early liturgical pieces. The *Acts of John* and *Acts of Thomas* contain prayers, hymns, and songs that reflect early Christian theological ideas. Quite a few apocryphal acts include scenes in which the apostles preach extended sermons or offer prayers to God. Some of these prayers parallel early creeds and give us insights into developments in early Christian worship, beliefs, and rituals.

These acts include some notable fantastical elements, too. For example, in the *Acts of John* the apostle stays at an inn and is bothered by bedbugs. John banishes the bugs with a command and they obediently wait outside the room until morning, when he allows them to return. The apostle poses an allegorical moral about obeying God, but this episode is even more striking because the Greek word for "bedbug" (*koreis*) sounds like the word for "girl" (*korai*). The story is, therefore, both entertaining and complicated, deserving of multiple interpretations.

Besides the five early acts, there are plenty of other texts about the apostles. Some of the apostles even had multiple acts written about them. In the Greek *Acts of Andrew and Matthias*, Matthias (or Matthew) is sent as a missionary to an island of cannibals (Mermedonians), but he is captured, blinded, imprisoned, and fattened for slaughter. God sends Andrew to rescue his friend. During the sea journey, the ship's captain (really Jesus in disguise) quizzes the apostle on the Christian faith, and Andrew relates some interesting noncanonical details about Jesus's life and teachings. Andrew arrives in Mermedonia, breaks Matthias out of prison and heals him, faces off against Satan, is tortured and imprisoned, escapes, brings a purgative flood to the city, and converts the cannibals to Christianity (along with a more balanced diet).

The *Acts of Thomas and His Wonderworking Skin* tells a story generally similar to the earlier *Acts of Thomas*, but it diverges in major details and expands the narrative. The most notable expansion is a series of miracles that Thomas performs after he is flayed, as he carries his skin with him on his travels in India. He uses his skin as a sort of healing blanket, performing resurrections that lead to many conversions.

It is possible that the *Wonderworking Skin* narrative was influenced by the *Acts of Bartholomew*, which relates another apostle's journey as a missionary to India. While there, Bartholomew challenges and defeats demons oppressing the local people, and much of this narrative concerns the defeat of pagan idolatry as the local people are converted to Christianity. There is a strong theme about theodicy, or the nature of human suffering and evil in the world. In some versions of this story, Bartholomew is martyred by flaying.

All of these acts and more are worth reading for a number of reasons. Although they provide entertaining narratives rich in fascinating details, they also represent early Christian ideas about the spread of Christianity and present narratives about saintly men and women that Christians have continued to venerate over the last few millennia.

Acts of Paul and Thecla

FACTS

Author:	Unknown
Date written:	Between about 170 and 200 CE
Language:	Greek
Canons:	None, but popular in various Christian communities, especially in Eastern Orthodox Christianity

DISCOVERY

Knowledge of this work in Eastern Greek Christianity begins in the late second century and continues to the present. Modern study of this work began when John Ernest Grabe published the first edition in 1698. Soon afterward, Johann Albert Fabricius published it in his collection of apocrypha in 1703. Since then, scholars have continued to discover manuscripts of other versions, including translations in Arabic, Armenian, Coptic, Ge'ez, Latin, Church Slavic, and Syriac.

SUMMARY

This narrative focuses on a young woman named Thecla, who is captivated by the apostle Paul's teachings and converts from paganism to Christianity because of them. Paul travels to Iconium (in modern-day Turkey) to spread the gospel, and while he preaches about the virtues of chastity, Thecla, a young virgin woman in a neighboring house, hears him and becomes enamored of his message. For days, Thecla does nothing but listen to Paul. Her mother, Theoclia, becomes concerned and sends for the man betrothed to Thecla, Thamyris.

Eventually, Thamyris becomes so enraged by Thecla's commitment to Paul's message that he stirs up other men who are angered by the women of Iconium joining Thecla in her commitment to chastity. Paul is imprisoned for this unrest. Thecla steals away to the prison and stays with Paul, listening to his teaching. When Paul and Thecla are discovered, the governor exiles Paul and sentences Thecla to be burned. When she is burned, however, God sends a storm that puts the fire out, and Thecla escapes.

Thecla meets up with Paul, and they travel together to Antioch. When they arrive, a nobleman named Alexander desires Thecla, but she scorns him. As revenge, Alexander leads Thecla before the governor, who condemns her to face wild beasts in the coliseum. The narrative includes a series of episodes in which Thecla faces wild beasts but remains unscathed—often because the beasts befriend her. For example, a lioness becomes her guardian and kills every other animal, until the lioness is mortally wounded while protecting Thecla. At the climax of these episodes, Thecla baptizes herself and is surrounded by a holy fire of protection. The governor recognizes God as Thecla's savior and releases her.

Thecla meets up with Paul again in Myra, but then she travels alone to Iconium, where she finds Thamyris dead but preaches to her mother. She travels to Seleucia (in present-day Iraq) and preaches the gospel there before her death.

In some manuscripts, Thecla lives out her days in a cave, thwarting men who try to rape and defile her. In one version, God saves her by creating an opening in the cave that she uses to escape. She lives until she is ninety years old. This same version praises Thecla as "the first martyr of God and apostle and virgin."

ANALYSIS

Although the *Acts of Paul and Thecla* circulated on its own, this work was part of the much-longer composite cycle known as the *Acts of Paul*. This narrative has many parallels with other Greek romance fictions from antiquity, and—like those works—a central issue of this narrative is gender and sexuality. Although Thecla falls in love with Paul, it is for his teaching and not for romantic or sexual reasons—in fact, she embraces chastity because of her greater love of God. Paul fades into the background as the rest of the story revolves around the consequences of Thecla's commitment to virginity and the lust of powerful men around her. This apocryphon is closely linked with the early cult of Saint Thecla, which began in Seleucia and quickly spread throughout the Near East and Mediterranean world, popularizing early Christian teachings about chastity, especially for young virgin women.

Acts of Thomas

FACTS

Author: Unknown; attributed to the apostle "Didymus" ("Twin") Judas Thomas, meant to be Jesus's twin brother

Date written: Between about 220 and 240 CE

Language: Probably Syriac, possibly Greek

Canons: None, but popular in various Christian communities, especially in Eastern Orthodox Christianity and the Assyrian Church of the East

DISCOVERY

Knowledge of this work in Eastern Christianity begins in the third century and continues to the present. Johann Albert Fabricius published a Latin version in his collection of apocrypha in 1703. Johannes Carolus Thilo published the first Greek edition in 1823. William Wright's edition of the Syriac version in 1871 was a substantial breakthrough. Since then, scholars have continued to discover manuscripts of other versions, including translations in Arabic, Armenian, Coptic, Ge'ez, Georgian, Latin, Church Slavic, and Syriac.

SUMMARY

After the apostles cast lots to determine where they will travel to spread the gospel, Thomas refuses to go to India as assigned. Jesus appears to the apostle during the night, but Thomas still refuses to go. Just then, a merchant named Abban comes looking to buy a carpenter to take to King Gundaphorus in India. Jesus sells Thomas to him as a slave, and the apostle's journey begins.

When Thomas and Abban arrive in India, they enter the city of Andrapolis during a wedding celebration for the king's only daughter. Thomas stands out for his odd behavior. He recites an enigmatic *Hymn of the Bride*, prays for the newlyweds, and teaches them to abstain from sex and choose celibacy.

Next, Thomas meets King Gundaphorus, who commissions the apostle to build a royal palace, but instead Thomas gives away the king's money to the poor. Enraged, Gundaphorus imprisons Thomas. The king's brother Gad dies and discovers that Thomas has built the palace in heaven; Gad's soul is sent back to his body, and he tells Gundaphorus, who frees Thomas and converts to Christianity.

The rest of the narrative includes stories about Thomas traveling around India performing miracles and spreading the gospel. These stories include encounters with demons who oppress women through sexual violence; a talking donkey; an evil sorcerer; and many sick and dead people healed and resurrected by Thomas. The narrative culminates in a series of episodes in which Thomas converts some women who then choose celibacy, but their husbands seek revenge. One of these men is King Misdaeus, who imprisons, tortures, and eventually kills Thomas. Yet, after the apostle's death, Misdaeus's son is tortured by a demon, and Thomas appears in a vision to heal the son, leading to the king's conversion.

Especially notable is the *Hymn of the Pearl*, a complex allegory about a son of a king who is sent to Egypt to retrieve a pearl from a dragon but forgets his mission along the way, until the king sends a letter to remind the boy and help him achieve his quest.

ANALYSIS

Many scholars attribute this and other early Christian works related to Thomas to a Syrian "School of Thomas." Such works share common themes, such as the rejection of materiality, sexuality, and bodily resurrection. We can compare "Gnostic" texts and the *Gospel of Thomas*, which is considered part of this Thomasine literature, and which the author of the *Acts of Thomas* used. Works attributed to the "School of Thomas" are related to veneration of this apostle by Christians in Syria and India, where Thomas Christians regard him as the apostle to their continent. Christians in those regions developed a particular veneration for Thomas, and a cult to the apostle persists from early Christianity to the present. While the whole of the *Acts of Thomas* is not usually categorized as "Gnostic," many scholars find gnostic elements in the *Hymn of the Pearl*, an earlier Syriac poem inserted into the narrative. This hymn is often interpreted as an allegory about the fate of the soul beyond its earthly existence in the material body, which it transcends upon death. This insertion represents how the *Acts* accumulated additions like speeches, prayers, and hymns with complex theological content.

OTHER APOSTOLIC TEXTS

The Didache

FACTS

Also known as: The Teaching, Teaching of the Twelve Apostles, Teaching of the Lord to the Gentiles by the Twelve Apostles

Author: Unknown; attributed to the apostles

Date written: Between about 70 and 150 CE

Language: Greek

Canons: None, although it was accepted as scripture by several early Christians

DISCOVERY

While early Christians mentioned or discussed the *Didache* (which many considered scriptural), it was largely unknown until the modern period. In 1873, Archbishop Philotheos Bryennios of Nicomedia discovered a version of the *Didache* in the eleventh-century Codex Hierosolymitanus (which also includes the *Letter of Barnabas*), in the Holy Church of the Sepulcher of

Constantinople, which he published in 1883. Other fragments in Greek, Coptic, Ge'ez, and Latin have also been discovered.

SUMMARY

This treatise begins (chapters 1–5) with a discussion of the "Two Ways," explained as "one of life" and "one of death." Starting off with a variation of the commandment to love God and love neighbors, the work then offers extended explication parallel to teachings in the Gospel of Matthew. The work then offers a series of other commandments of the "Way of Life," many from the Decalogue (Ten Commandments). Some of this section parallels Jewish wisdom literature and Jesus's Beatitudes in Matthew. The section ends with a discussion of the "Way of Death" through spiritual vices.

The second section (chapters 6–10) gives instructions for daily and ecclesiastical rituals. These include guidelines about food, baptism, fasts, prayer, the Eucharist, and thanksgiving. This section contains an early form of the Lord's Prayer (as in Matthew 6:9–13).

The next section (chapters 11–15) provides instructions about church leadership, like the ways to treat apostles and prophets, and the appointment of bishops and deacons.

Finally, the treatise ends (chapter 16) with an eschatological conclusion that incorporates apocalyptic imagery and themes. The work warns about false prophets, lawlessness, persecution, an Antichrist figure, and a final judgment.

ANALYSIS

This work is a composite, developed over several decades as older and newer material was combined. The oldest portions are probably parts of the "Two Ways" section in chapters 1–5 and some ancient liturgical traditions in chapters 6–10. Other pieces were added over time as the need for further instruction emerged.

The "Two Ways" was a common idea in early Jewish literature, such as works found among the Dead Sea Scrolls, like the

Community Rule (page 53). It also appears in the *Letter of Barnabas* (page 106), which probably used the same source as the *Didache*.

This work is a particularly significant witness to early Christian rituals and church order. These include everyday observances as well as baptism (as practiced by some early Jews, as in the Essene community) and thanksgiving meals linked to the Eucharist. Similarly, this work shows the emergence of a two-part hierarchy of leaders. All of this shows how early Christian authors sought to work out not only theology but also practical applications of Christian life in the late first and early second centuries.

A number of images and themes share parallels with canonical early Christian writings. Much of the *Didache* is similar to teachings in the Gospel of Matthew, while images in the final section resonate with passages from the prophetic books of the Hebrew Bible and other eschatological and apocalyptic passages in the New Testament. Many parallels echo early Jewish literature, leading some scholars to focus on the *Didache* as evidence of a Jewish-Christian author seeking to synthesize older traditions with emerging rituals.

Letter of the Apostles

FACTS

Author:	Unknown; attributed to the apostles
Date written:	Between about 150 and 200 CE
Language:	Probably Greek, but it survives in full only in Ge'ez
Canons:	None, but it is held in high regard by Orthodox Tewahedo Christians

DISCOVERY

In 1895, while in Cairo, Carl Schmidt discovered a fragmentary book from the fourth or fifth century with the Coptic text of the *Letter of the Apostles*. Josef Bick published a fragment of a fifth-century Latin version in 1908. The major break-through for knowledge of this work came in 1913, when Louis Guerrier and Sylvain Grébault published an edition of the full text in Ge'ez, based on the discovery of several previously unknown manuscripts.

SUMMARY

Although this work is introduced as a letter from the apostles, it exhibits many generic features of gospels and apocalypses. The first part (chapters 1–10) relates Jesus's birth, life, death, and resurrection—a lot of which parallels the canonical gospels. The second section (chapters 11–50) includes a visionary dialogue between the risen Christ and the apostles before the Ascension.

Much of the dialogue focuses on eschatological issues like Jesus's Second Coming and the Last Judgment. Of specific concern is the exact time of Jesus's return, which he claims will take place 150 years after this vision. While the apostles press Jesus with specific theological questions (sometimes a humorous amount), Jesus teaches them many details about the resurrection of the soul and body. Jesus recounts his descent into hell after his crucifixion, when he preached to the patriarchs and prophets, offering them "the right hand of the baptism of life."

After this account, Jesus shifts to telling the apostles about Paul, highlighting his persecution of Christians, conversion, and teachings to come. Paul's mission, Jesus intimates, is the beginning of the signs of the Second Coming, and the following passage includes an apocalyptic discourse about the portents of the Last Judgment. When the apostles anxiously express their concern about the fate of those who will be punished, Jesus gives them guidance for teaching the gospel and baptizing believers. Jesus ends this section with exhortations to preach to rich and poor alike, with a final warning about heretics.

The text concludes with a brief account of Jesus's ascension into heaven.

ANALYSIS

Notably, the *Letter of the Apostles* contains many of the theological positions that later came to be upheld as orthodox. It relies on the canonical gospels (especially John) and other New Testament texts, as well as the *Letter of Barnabas* and the *Shepherd of Hermas*. It is also related to other apocrypha, as a brief reference to Jesus teaching his teacher with the Hebrew alphabet is parallel to the *Infancy Gospel of Thomas* (page 73); and some of its apocalyptic imagery is parallel to works like the *Apocalypse of Peter* (page 119) and the *Apocalypse of Paul* (page 121).

This work is explicitly anti-Gnostic. Many of the questions that the apostles ask indicate the author's knowledge of and reaction to ideas found in works categorized as "Gnostic" texts. The manner of Jesus's teaching challenges notions about "secret" teachings (like gnosis), since he encourages the apostles to travel and preach this information to all who will listen and believe. More specifically, the work refutes two figures by name: Cerinthus (fl. 50–100 CE), who was condemned as a "Gnostic" heretic; and Simon, probably the figure confronted by Peter in Acts 8:9–24. These specific names seem to represent all heretics, especially those deemed "Gnostics" by early Christians, since there is a general anxiety throughout this work about heresy.

Letter of Barnabas

FACTS

Author:	Unknown; attributed to Barnabas, the apostle Paul's companion
Date written:	Between about 70 and 135 CE
Language:	Greek
Canons:	None, although it was accepted as scripture by several early Christians and is included in the fourth-century Bible known as the Codex Sinaiticus

DISCOVERY

Clement of Alexandria (who considered the apocryphon scriptural) quotes many passages from the *Letter of Barnabas* throughout his *Stromata*, providing an important witness from early Christianity. In 1844, Constantin von Tischendorf visited Saint Catherine's Monastery in Egypt and discovered a fourth-century Greek Bible known as the Codex Sinaiticus, containing the entire Septuagint, deuterocanonical works, New Testament, and (at the end) the *Letter of Barnabas* and *Shepherd of Hermas*. He published the text in 1862. In 1873, Archbishop Philotheos Bryennios of Nicomedia discovered another version of the *Letter* in the eleventh-century Codex Hierosolymitanus (which also includes the *Didache*), in the Holy Church of the Sepulcher of Constantinople, which he published in 1883. Other fragments in Greek, Latin, and Syriac have also been discovered.

SUMMARY

The central aim of this letter is to impart "perfect knowledge," summed up as "hope of life," "righteousness," and "love of joy and happiness." Each one of these is stated in the first chapter and each governs a section of the letter.

The first few chapters concern rituals like sacrifices and fasting, but this section culminates in an eschatological apocalyptic reflection. Much of what follows is framed by this eschatology, as the author discusses Israel's failure to follow the covenant. The central section of this treatise focuses on Christ's passion on the cross, bolstered by references to the foreshadowing of Christ in the Hebrew scriptures, especially the Law and the Prophets. All of this culminates in discussion of Christians as the true heirs of the covenant, the sabbath, and the destruction of the Second Temple.

The last section discusses the "Two Ways" and commandments for following the way of life. Many of these are drawn from the Decalogue (Ten Commandments). The Way of Darkness is contrasted as a path of vices.

The treatise concludes with an exhortation to follow the Lord's commandments in order to be righteous and find glory in the kingdom of God through resurrection, again within the framework of an eschatological outlook looking forward to the Judgment Day.

ANALYSIS

As part of the works of the Apostolic Fathers, the *Letter* is not always considered among apocrypha, but it does have a claim to this status because it was attributed to Barnabas (the apostle Paul's companion) and included in the fourth-century Codex Sinaiticus. Like the *Didache* (page 102), which probably used the same source, this letter focuses quite a bit on the "Two Ways," a common concept in early Jewish literature. The author uses dualist imagery like life and death, light and darkness. We can compare some of these ideas to texts from the Dead Sea Scrolls, like the *Community Rule* (page 53) and certain aspects of dualism in the *War Scroll* (page 60). Yet the author demonstrates anxieties about distinguishing Christianity from Judaism, with some ideas exhibiting anti-Jewish attitudes. This is most prominent in the discussion of Israel abandoning the covenant.

The significant focus on knowledge in this letter indicates some overlap with the intense interest in gnosis found throughout "Gnostic" texts. Some scholars believe that the letter manifests early elements that are more fully represented in later texts categorized as "Gnostic." Nonetheless, the knowledge in this work is meant for righteous living rather than spiritual transcendence. All of this points toward living the Way of Life in preparation for God's judgment.

Letter of Pseudo-Titus

FACTS

Also known as: *Epistle of (Pseudo-) Titus, Pseudo-Titus Epistle*
Author: Unknown; attributed to Titus, the apostle
 Paul's disciple

Date written: Between about 400 and 500 CE
Language: Latin
Canons: None

DISCOVERY

This letter survives in only one eighth-century handwritten copy, in the Würzburg Universitätsbibliothek (manuscript M.p.th.f. 28), probably from Bavaria. The manuscript contains a number of religious works, many for preaching. Germain Morin discovered the manuscript in 1896, and Donatien de Bruyne edited the *Letter* in 1925.

SUMMARY

The *Letter of Pseudo-Titus* is stylized as a letter from Paul's disciple Titus, written to a community of ascetic men and women about the virtues of chastity and the vices of sex. The letter begins with a discussion of the promises that the Lord gives to those who adhere to holiness and purity.

Next, the letter addresses women as virgins, rewards for those who remain chaste in life, and punishments for those who do not. The letter then shifts to address both men and women briefly before turning back to women in a series of metaphors for the body based on holy buildings. The letter shifts again to address men by offering a warning about the dangers of desire, the problems of lust in the heart as adultery, a series of examples of holy men from the Hebrew Bible, and the solution to temptations of the body through solitary asceticism.

These exhortations are followed by relating the consequences of men's behavior for the entire community, an apocalyptic vision of eschatological punishments for those who do not remain pure, a return to asceticism as the solution, and a series of negative examples from the Hebrew Bible. With another shift to a more general address, the text again relates the communal consequences of unchaste behavior before turning to a conclusion about the heavenly rewards for those who remain chaste.

ANALYSIS

The core concern of this letter is that the author's audience has faltered in their vows of celibacy, engaging in practices like "spiritual marriage" and sexual relationships within their community. Throughout the letter, the author alludes to and quotes many passages from the Bible and other apocrypha. In particular, examples of figures used in the letter derive from apocryphal narratives like the *Acts of Andrew*, *John*, *Paul and Thecla*, and a story about Peter and his daughter preserved in the Coptic *Acts of Peter* and the *Acts of Nereus and Achilleus*.

OTHER APOSTOLIC TEXTS

Letter to the Laodiceans

This work purports to be the letter written by the apostle Paul to the church at Laodicea (in modern-day Turkey), as mentioned in Colossians 4:16. Early Christians knew about a work with this same title, but it is unclear if it was this one or another lost forgery. The work is a compilation of verses from the canonical Pauline letters, especially Philippians and Galatians. It does not have a coherent message, but is a pastiche of encouragements and exhortations about Paul's life, prayer, rejoicing in God, belief in Christ, eternal life, and keeping the faith. This letter survives only in Latin, and it was composed sometime before about 400 CE, since Jerome knew it. Pope Gregory the Great and some medieval authors considered it to be canonical; it circulated in many witnesses to the Latin Vulgate in the Middle Ages.

Letters between Paul and Seneca

Fourteen letters written as if between the apostle Paul and the Roman moralist Seneca survive, composed in Latin probably in the fourth century CE. The main point of the letters is to situate the value (or superiority) of Christian philosophy in relation to pagan philosophy. The collection demonstrates the merging of ideas represented across early Christian literature, as authors synthesized concepts from Jewish, Hellenistic, and Roman cultures. Jerome and Augustine knew these letters, and they were popular throughout the Middle Ages, with many medieval authors believing them to be genuine, though not canonical.

CHAPTER EIGHT

Revelations and Apocalypses

T he genre of literature known as "apocalypse" is a particular type of writing that
emerged in Second Temple Judaism
(between the construction of the Second Temple
in 516 BCE and its destruction by the Romans in
70 CE) and was carried over into early Christianity.
The Greek term *apocalypse* means "uncovering,"
used to indicate a revelation of divine knowledge.
Often, apocalyptic literature is framed as prophetic
messages given through supernatural dreams and
visions. The canonical book of the Revelation of
John (also known as the Apocalypse of John) is one
example of this kind of work, but many more have
been composed over the centuries, beginning in
early Judaism.

The roots of early Jewish apocalypses rest in
a synthesis of ideas from different ancient Near
Eastern cultures, including:

- Prophetic revelation
- Wisdom literature
- Babylonian, Persian, Egyptian, and
  Syrian materials
- Hellenistic ideas
- Folk traditions

All of these influences combined to create a unique and prominent form of literature that developed in early Judaism, was taken up by early Christians, and spread as Christianity did. In addition to these influences, a major characteristic of apocalyptic literature is an expression of anxiety about current events, and especially resistance to empire, as seen in early Judaism and early Christianity.

Apocalypses usually include various common elements, like a revelation to the narrator, who passes on that revelation to readers; a narrative frame that holds the pieces together; a supernatural guide, like an angel; a tour of otherworldly locations; and divine secrets about the cosmos. Many scholars have emphasized that at the core of apocalypses is a worldview of apocalypticism, which attempts to understand present, earthly circumstances in relation to the supernatural cosmos. Especially prominent is a focus on eschatology, or concerns about human life, death, the afterlife, judgment, and the final fate of human souls. As we will see, these are just a few of the fascinating ideas threaded throughout apocryphal apocalypses.

Jewish apocalyptic literature was well established by the time the Qumran community established themselves, and a number of works in the Dead Sea Scrolls contain apocalyptic content (see chapter 4). This is particularly true of the *Community Rule* (page 53) and the *War Scroll* (page 60). Some scholars have seen the apocalyptic elements in these works and other writings in the Dead Sea Scrolls as evidence for a deep-seated apocalypticism in the Qumran community.

We find elements of apocalyptic literature throughout early Christian writings, including the canonical Gospels, Paul's letters, and many other works like the *Didache* (page 102), the *Letter of the Apostles* (page 104), and the *Letter of Barnabas* (page 106). Among the Nag Hammadi Codices found in Egypt are a number of apocalyptic works (see chapter 6, where the *Apocalypse of Adam* was considered, page 93). Most notable of these are the Coptic *Apocalypse of Peter* and the Coptic *Apocalypse of Paul* (not to be confused with the works with similar names discussed in this chapter). These works share common characteristics with other apocalypses as well as concerns of gnosticism, like the dualism between material existence and spiritual reality. As other Christian literature attests, apocalypses continued to remain popular over the centuries—just as apocalyptic ideas continue to remain popular in our own time.

1 Enoch

FACTS

Also known as: Book of Enoch
Author: Various unknown Palestinian Jews; attributed to Enoch
Date written: In stages from about 300 BCE onward, compiled together between about 100 BCE and 100 CE
Language: Probably Aramaic, or possibly Hebrew; it survives in full form only in Ge'ez, translated from Greek
Canons: Beta Israel, Orthodox Tewahedo

DISCOVERY

Some early Christians accepted *1 Enoch* as scripture, but it was known only partially or by reputation in most Christian communities until the modern period. This work did survive as part of the Ethiopian Jewish and Christian traditions, and the Scottish traveler James Bruce brought back from Ethiopia three manuscripts of the work in 1773. Antoine Isaac Silvestre de Sacy printed portions of the Ethiopian text in 1800. Richard Laurence published a translation in 1821 and the first full edition in 1838. Fragments in Aramaic were found among the Dead Sea Scrolls. Fragmentary versions also survive in Greek and Latin.

SUMMARY

The premise of *1 Enoch* is the verse in Genesis 5:24 that says that "God took" Enoch, a descendant of Adam and Eve and ancestor of Noah. In this work, the passage about the end of Enoch's life is interpreted as his being taken on a journey that revealed to him the mysteries of the universe. The composite book of *1 Enoch* is organized in five major sections, with subsections that may be broken down within them:

- Book of the Watchers (1–36)
  - Introductory chapters (1–5)
- Similitudes of Enoch (37–71)
- Astronomical Book (72–82)
- Dream Visions (83–90)
- Epistle of Enoch (91–107)
  - Apocalypse of Weeks (91:12–17; 93:1–10)
  - *Book of Noah* (106–107)
- Conclusion (108)

The first part includes a discourse on the judgment of the righteous and the wicked, as well as an introduction to Enoch's vision, followed by a narrative about the fall of the Watchers (as in Genesis 6:1–4), who fornicated with humans and fathered the Nephilim. Most of this book depicts Enoch's tours of the earth, Sheol (the Jewish underworld), and heaven. Much of this concerns lore about the angels, like the names and roles of archangels and luminaries in the heavens.

The Similitudes include a series of depictions focused on eschatological subjects like judgment of the righteous and the wicked; lore about angels, including the fallen angels; depictions of the Messiah, known as the Son of Man, Righteous One, and Elect One; secrets of the cosmos; Eden, Paradise, and heaven; and the resurrection of the dead.

As its name implies, the third major section deals with astronomical lore within the framework of a solar calendar. It contains detailed information about the heavenly bodies as well as discussion of the sun and moon in relation to elements of the earth.

The Dream Visions reveal biblical history, covering narratives about Israel up to the Maccabees. This section is full of allegorical symbolism, especially animal imagery. The Apocalypse of Weeks continues this narrative revelation of time, as it concerns events of the world over ten periods of weeks leading up to the Last Judgment. The *Book of Noah* fits into this revelation of history, with an account of Noah's life and the Flood.

Finally, the conclusion features another vision about judgment, ending with an emphasis on a generation of light who represent the righteous.

ANALYSIS

The book of *1 Enoch* is a particular example of an early Jewish apocalypse that influenced many later authors in Judaism and Christianity. As with many apocalypses, an obvious major concern in this work is eschatology, especially the nature of judgment for the wicked and the righteous. The concept of judgment unites both the accounts of Israelite history in the past and depictions of eschatological consequences in the future. One theme is the punishment of the rich who overlook the needs of the oppressed. The places that Enoch visits emphasize the theme of judgment, since he sees the mountain where God sits as a judge over the earth, the afterlife (Sheol) where the dead wait for judgment, and places of rewards and punishments for the righteous and the wicked.

1 Enoch presents a complicated textual history, since it is a composite of different pieces composed at different times. The work therefore represents a corpus of literature interested in Enoch that developed over time. The present form was compiled by a Jew or perhaps an early Christian around the time of Jesus's life. Various parts were clearly influential on other early Jewish authors, since many of the same ideas in other apocryphal works are derived from this one. There is evidence that *1 Enoch* was known to some of the authors of New Testament works, and a passage from 1:9 is directly cited and quoted in Jude 1:14–15.

2 Esdras

FACTS

Also known as: 4 Ezra

Author: An unknown Palestinian Jew, with later additions by Christians; attributed to Ezra

Date written:	Around 100 CE, with additions in the second and third centuries CE
Language:	Hebrew or possibly Aramaic (lost), translated into Greek (lost) and from Greek into Latin and other languages in which it now survives
Canons:	Beta Israel, Orthodox Tewahedo. It was included in certain manuscripts of the Latin Vulgate during the Middle Ages

DISCOVERY

The Latin version was widespread and popular in Western Europe throughout the Middle Ages and well into the modern period. It has been printed many times by scholars, including by Johann Albert Fabricius in his collection of pseudepigrapha in 1713. Other versions (some only fragmentary) survive in Arabic, Armenian, Coptic, Ge'ez, Georgian, and Syriac.

SUMMARY

This apocalypse is stylized as a revelation to Ezra, the biblical prophet who led the Jews back to their homeland after their exile in Babylon. After an introduction that presents Ezra's genealogy and prophetic call, there is a prophetic speech about God's mercies, Israel's rejection of God, and God's judgment upon Israel. Then follow seven visions mediated to Ezra. The first vision contains a discourse between the prophet and an angel about the judgment of Israel, the coming of a new age, and the apocalyptic signs of the new age. The second vision includes more discourse on the new age and more signs of its inauguration.

The third vision focuses on eschatological judgment for the righteous and the wicked, Ezra's sympathy for the wicked who will be punished, and the contrast between God's mercy and justice. It again ends with signs of the new age.

The fourth vision diverges from the previous visions, including a depiction of a woman in mourning for a lost son, transformed into Zion. The fifth vision follows, offering an allegory about an eagle rising from the sea, interpreted by Ezra as the Roman Empire, which will be punished for the persecution of the Jews. The sixth vision portrays a man rising from the sea to destroy his enemies. The final vision relates an angel giving God's message to Ezra, who dictates it to five men over forty days, resulting in them recording ninety-four books—twenty-four books for the public and another seventy books of hidden knowledge for only the wise.

The last few chapters (added later) include a series of denunciations of the wicked and those opposed to God's justice, with a final promise of God's deliverance for the righteous.

ANALYSIS

2 Esdras is composite, made up of three distinct units: the core, *4 Ezra* (chapters 3–14), to which were added *5 Ezra* (chapters 1–2) and *6 Ezra* (chapters 15–16). This apocalypse is one of several apocryphal works concerning the prophet Ezra.

In addition to the biblical books of Ezra and Nehemiah (also called 1–2 Ezra), he is the main figure of a Greek Jewish apocryphon titled *3 Ezra* (accepted as canonical by Eastern Orthodox and Orthodox Tewahedo Christians). The titles of these different works explain the alternative title of *2 Esdras* and its component parts.

The section known as *4 Ezra* was likely composed by a Palestinian Jew writing in response to the Roman siege of Jerusalem and destruction of the temple; the date is established by indication of the first vision taking place "in the thirtieth year after the destruction of our city"—that is, 100 CE. The other sections were added by Christians reworking the apocalypse in the second and third centuries. This work represents the synthetic adaptation of earlier Jewish literature in the early Christian period.

A major theme aligning this work with other early Jewish works about Ezra is judgment. The visions revolve around God's judgment over Israel and eschatological judgment of individual souls. The work explores the tensions between judgment and mercy, in terms of both theodicy and eschatology, and emphasizes individual and collective righteousness.

The last vision includes an important witness to the concept of twenty-four books in the Hebrew Bible as well as acknowledgment of many other apocryphal works that contain hidden knowledge. This situates the book of *2 Esdras* within a corpus of early Jewish literature that is legitimized with the notion that God ordained these works as a sort of second canon.

Apocalypse of Peter

FACTS

Author:	Unknown; attributed to the apostle Peter
Date written:	Between about 100 and 150 CE
Language:	Greek, but it survives in full only in Ge'ez
Canons:	None, but it was popular among various early Christian communities before it was suppressed over concerns about orthodoxy

DISCOVERY

Clement of Alexandria knew this work and considered it to be scripture, and it enjoyed some popularity between the second and fifth centuries, but it fell into obscurity after that. The leaves of a Greek book containing this apocalypse were discovered in the grave of a Christian monk in Akhmim, Egypt, during excavations by Gaston Maspéro in 1886–1887. Urbain Bouriant published these fragments in 1892. In 1907 and 1910, Sylvain Grébaut published a full version of the work in Ge'ez.

SUMMARY

The *Apocalypse of Peter* contains a revelation to the apostle Peter of the afterlife, including both heaven and hell. It begins with Peter's descent into hell, containing fires and pits of torment, where he sees sinners punished according to their sins. Among these are blasphemers hung over fire by their tongues; adulterous women hung by their hair and their male consorts hung by their loins; murderers tormented by beasts while their victims watch; homosexuals and lesbians cast off a cliff; women who force abortions swallowed up to their necks in a river of excrement, blood, and gore, and tormented by the spirits of their unborn children; slanderers forced to gnaw on their tongues; the rich who ignore widows and single mothers cast onto a pillar of fire with spikes; idolators bound in chains of fire before their idols; sorcerers and sorceresses hung on wheels of fire. Other general punishments, such as assorted torments, burning in fire, and being submerged in rivers of fire, are mentioned for different unspecified sins—all according to the deeds of sinners in life.

In contrast, the depiction of heaven is shorter and less elaborate. The righteous are described as beautiful, with white skin and curly hair, and they wear clothes of light. There are abundant flowers and spices, like a paradise. All those in this paradise join in choral prayer in worship of God.

ANALYSIS

This apocalypse is considered to be the earliest surviving extended depiction of heaven and hell in a Christian work. In fact, the author was more interested in hell than in heaven. Punishments for sinners usually fit the sins. Much of this, it seems, is meant to evoke penitence from those still alive, in order to spur them to repentance and change. The work continually emphasizes to readers that now (while still alive) is the time to repent.

It is clear that the author of this apocalypse was influenced by Jewish apocalyptic works, like *1 Enoch* (page 114) and *2 Esdras* (page 116), as well as apocalyptic elements of the canonical Gospel of Matthew. Although this work later lost its relevance, it was influential on other Christian apocalypses. Many scholars believe that the author of the *Apocalypse of Paul* (page 121) drew upon the *Apocalypse of Peter* for inspiration, even using specific imagery and depictions of torments for sinners. It is also possible that the author of the *Acts of Thomas* (page 100) drew on this apocalypse for a depiction of hell in that work.

Apocalypse of Paul

FACTS

Author: Unknown; attributed to the apostle Paul

Date written: Between about 250 and 300 CE; Latin translation
between about 440 and 520 CE

Language: Greek, but Latin versions are significant witnesses

Canons: None, but it was wildly popular across various Eastern and Western Christian communities, as well as
in Beta Israel Judaism

DISCOVERY

The *Apocalypse of Paul* was widespread and popular across
Christian communities throughout the Middle Ages and into
the modern period. Johann Albert Fabricius published it in his
collection of apocrypha in 1703, and Constantin von Tischendorf
published it in a collection of apocryphal apocalypses in 1866.
Versions survive in Armenian, Greek, Coptic, Ge'ez, Latin, Church
Slavic, and Syriac.

SUMMARY

The premise of this apocalypse (like others with similar titles) is
the apostle Paul's comments in 2 Corinthians 12:1–5 about a man
(here Paul himself) being taken up into the heavens and learning
certain secrets. The "Long Latin" version is especially significant
for its inclusion of an extended prologue about how the book was
found at the city of Tarsus, when an angel prompted a nobleman to
dig up the foundations of his house, and the man discovered a box
containing a copy of the text along with Paul's sandals.

    The apocalypse proper begins with a depiction of the sun, moon,
stars, waters, and earth crying out in protest against humanity. In
every case, God answers that he knows all, and remains patient for
repentance, but that if humans do not return to him, he will judge

them. Next, angels appear before God at sunrise and sunset to give him reports about the deeds of the humans they watch over.

Paul is then led by an angel to begin his tour of heaven and hell. Paul looks down at the world and witnesses the fate of souls after death. He sees a soul leave its body, and it is put on trial: The person's deeds are put on display and angels testify for and against the person before the soul is taken before God for judgment. The souls of the righteous are commended, sent to the archangel Michael, and taken to Paradise with celebration; the souls of the wicked are admonished, claimed by demons, and taken to hell with mourning.

Paul tours three heavens, each with different souls of the righteous. In the second heaven is a land of promise with a river of milk and honey and trees symbolizing purity. The angel then leads Paul through the City of Christ, with twelve walls, twelve towers, and twelve gates, as well as four rivers of honey, milk, wine, and oil, each dividing a region for a different category of the righteous.

The angel next leads Paul through hell, which is divided into regions for different sinners. These regions include rivers of fire, pits of torture, walls of fire, and a place of ice and snow. Among the sinners are those who are neither hot nor cold in their belief; have inappropriate discussions after the Eucharist; slander one another in church; plot against neighbors; dispense magical charms; commit adultery; defile virgins; harm orphans, widows, and the poor; break fasts; engage in homosexual or lesbian acts; and undergo abortions. A section in the middle discusses punishments for priests, bishops, deacons, and lectors who do not perform their duties or remain pure. Paul sees a worm that never rests and men and women in the cold for their denial of Christ's resurrection. Paul witnesses a vision of twenty-four elders and four beasts, after which Christ descends, the damned beg for mercy, and Christ responds to them by granting a Sunday respite from their punishments.

At last, Paul is led to Paradise, where he sees the origin of the four rivers. He then meets the Virgin Mary, the Israelite patriarchs and prophets, Zechariah and John the Baptist, then Abel, and finally Adam.

ANALYSIS

Much of the theology of this work is focused on the consequences of human actions for eschatological judgment. There is a particular concern with the responsibilities and righteousness of bishops, priests, deacons, and lectors. By the third and fourth centuries, all of these figures were significant leaders of Christian communities and integral to regular worship and administering sacraments like baptism and the Eucharist. In fact, the apocalypse exhibits related anxieties about the proper observance of the Eucharist, particularly the need for purity around the sacrament. Many of the condemned sins point to an increasing concern for certain forms of social justice in Christianity: rejection of usury, the virtue of almsgiving, as well as care for widows, orphans, strangers, pilgrims, and neighbors.

There is also an intense concern for the balance between judgment and mercy. Several times, Paul asks about the fairness in punishments for the sinful, and the angel continually reminds him that God is just and knows all. Even the form of the work is structured around balance between contrasts like the righteous and wicked, virtues and vices, rewards and punishments. All of this is meant to demonstrate God's divine foreknowledge, grace, mercy, and righteousness in judgment.

Apocalypse of Thomas

FACTS

Author: Unknown
Date written: Between about 200 and 400 CE
Language: Probably Latin
Canons: None, but the work was popular in Western Europe during the Middle Ages

DISCOVERY

Although this work enjoyed some widespread popularity in medieval Western Europe, it was relatively unknown to modern scholars until the twentieth century, except for a note of condemnation in the *Pseudo-Gelasian Decretal*. Friedrich Wilhelm first published a version of the text from a single manuscript in 1907, and Josef Bick published another version in 1908—though neither identified the text as the *Apocalypse of Thomas*. Soon afterward, Edmund Hauler and Ernst von Dobschütz correctly identified the text, and from that time onward other versions have been published.

SUMMARY

This apocalypse is made up of a revelation given by Christ to the apostle Thomas depicting events leading up to and occurring on Judgment Day. The work begins with disasters like famine, war, earthquakes, and diseases, followed by a focus on human sins like blasphemy, hate, and pride. Then the work relates the rise of a series of kings, some good and some evil. Heavenly portents are related, leading to the rise of the Antichrist. In contrast, events leading up to the Second Coming of Jesus are depicted, encompassing signs occurring on the seven days before the Last Judgment. These signs include a rain of blood, heaven's gates opening, the abyss opening, an earthquake, an eclipse, heavenly bodies ceasing to work, people fleeing from angels, war of the angels, and deliverance of the elect.

Finally, angels prepare the way for the appearance of Christ in the clouds with light. Heaven is unlocked to let out the souls of the saints, who return to their bodies for the resurrection of the dead from their graves. The righteous receive clothes of eternal life and are received into heaven, while the wicked are sent into the abyss.

ANALYSIS

This apocalypse concentrates on the eschatology of the Last Judgment. For the most part, the scope is on general judgment, with little about the fate of individual souls. Much of the imagery is natural or cosmic, although some of the signs are meant to correlate with earthly politics. Some manuscripts include added details, like prophecies meant to situate the apocalypse in relation to historical events. The imagery draws on previous works, like Revelation and other Jewish and Christian apocalypses. It was a major influence on later apocalyptic works in the medieval period, like legends about the Antichrist.

Other Apocalyptic Traditions

Many other Jewish and Christian apocalyptic works survive. In fact, apocalypses have been some of the most popular types of apocryphal literature over the centuries. The following works are especially worthy of note.

THE SHEPHERD OF HERMAS

Although this work of the Apostolic Fathers is usually not considered among apocrypha (mainly because it is not associated with a known biblical figure), it was both accepted as scripture by several early Christians and included in the fourth-century Bible known as the Codex Sinaiticus (along with the *Letter of Barnabas*). The *Shepherd* was composed in Greek between about 70 and 175 CE, in stages, and attributed to a former slave named Hermas, possibly a reference to the man mentioned in Romans 16:14. It contains a series of five apocalyptic revelations, followed by twelve commandments and ten parables in a visionary framework. The whole work is highly allegorical, but certain parts present interpretations provided by a mediating angel.

THE APOCALYPSE OF PSEUDO-METHODIUS

This work presents a revelation about human history from Adam and Eve through the spread of Islam and the End Times, leading up to the Final Judgment. It was composed in Syriac between about 685 and 690 CE by an unknown Christian and attributed to the fourth-century bishop and martyr Methodius of Olympus. Versions survive in Greek, Latin, and Church Slavic. Its most prominent imagery includes the invasion of Gog and Magog, the life of the Antichrist, a savior figure known as the Last World Emperor, and tribulations preceding the Second Coming of Christ and the Final Judgment. This apocalypse particularly exhibits anxieties about the spread of Islam in the Near East. It exerted widespread influence in the Middle Ages, especially concerning Christian-Muslim relations and anti-Muslim attitudes leading up to the Crusades, which began in the late eleventh century.

THE FIFTEEN SIGNS BEFORE JUDGMENT DAY

This work presents the signs that will occur on the fifteen days leading up to the Last Judgment. These include the rising of the seas, burning of the seas, leveling of the waters and earth, bloody dew, destruction of buildings, battling rocks, a great earthquake, falling stars, resurrection of the dead, and burning of the earth. Some versions claim that this text was found in Hebrew annals and translated by Jerome. Versions survive in Latin, Hebrew, Armenian, and many other European languages, but it is difficult to establish the original language (though Latin is the likeliest) or date. It circulated widely in Western Europe from about 1100 CE onward as one of the most popular works of any genre in medieval Western Europe. It survives in more than 600 manuscript copies, as well as many artistic depictions.

APPENDIX A: TIMELINE

586 BCE	Conquest of Palestine and Destruction of the First Temple by the Babylonian King Nebuchadnezzar; widespread dispersion (diaspora) of the Israelite people beyond Palestine
586–539 BCE	Babylonian Exile of the Israelite people in Babylonia
539–530 BCE	Reign of the Persian king Cyrus the Great over much of the Near East, including Babylonia and Palestine; he allowed the Israelite people to return from exile to Palestine in 539 BCE
515 BCE	Construction of the Second Temple, beginning the era known as "Second Temple Judaism"
333/2 BCE	Conquest of Palestine by the Greek Alexander the Great
ca. 250–50 BCE	Translation of the Hebrew Bible and deuterocanonical books into the Greek Septuagint
ca. 250 BCE– 100 CE	Canon of Hebrew Bible established
200 BCE	Conquest of Palestine by the Seleucid King Antiochus III the Great
167–160 BCE	Maccabean Revolt of Jews against the Seleucid Empire, under Antiochus IV Epiphanes
164–63 BCE	Rule of Judea under the Hasmonean Dynasty
63 BCE	Beginning of rule of Judea under the Roman Empire

ca. 4 BCE–30 CE	Life of Jesus of Nazareth
66–73 CE	Great Revolt of Jews against the Roman Empire, first of the Jewish-Roman Wars
70 CE	Destruction of the Second Temple
ca. 100–150 CE	*Bryennios List* composed, one of the earliest definitive lists of canonical books in the Hebrew Bible
115–117 CE	Kitos War, second of the Jewish-Roman Wars
132–136 CE	Bar Kokhba Revolt, third and final of the Jewish-Roman Wars
ca. 200 CE	*Baba Bathra* composed, with a list of the canonical books in the Hebrew Bible
325 CE	Council of Nicea (first ecumenical council), resulting in the repudiation of Arianism and creation of the *Nicene Creed*
367 CE	Athanasius of Alexandria composes his *39th Festal Letter* (in Greek), including an authoritative list of canonical books in the New Testament as it came to be observed in Eastern Orthodox and Roman Catholic communities
381 CE	Council of Constantinople (second ecumenical council), resulting in the repudiation of Arianism and Macedonianism and revision of the *Nicene Creed*
382 CE	Council of Rome, meeting of Catholic Church officials under the authority of Pope Damasus I, to affirm the contents of the canonical Christian Bible
382–405 CE	Jerome translates the Hebrew Bible and Greek New Testament into Latin (later called the Vulgate)

431 CE	Council of Ephesus (third ecumenical council), resulting in repudiation of Nestorianism and Pelagianism and proclamation of the Virgin Mary as "Theotokos" ("God-bearer," "Mother of God")
451 CE	Council of Chalcedon (fourth ecumenical council), resulting in repudiation of monophysitism, adoption of the Chalcedonian Creed, and schism of the Oriental Orthodox Churches from ecumenical unity
ca. 519–553 CE	*Pseudo-Gelasian Decree* composed, with a definitive list of canonical books in the Christian Bible and a list of works condemned as apocrypha
ca. 600–1000 CE	Masoretic Text of the Hebrew Bible established
1054 CE	East–West Schism, or the Great Schism, breaking ecumenical unity between Eastern Orthodox and Roman Catholic churches
1517 CE	Beginning of the Protestant Reformation in Europe
1546 CE	Council of Trent to define the Christian biblical canon
1582–1610 CE	Publication of the Douay-Rheims translation of the Latin Vulgate into English
1611 CE	Publication of the King James Version of the Bible in English translation
1945 CE	Discovery of the Nag Hammadi Codices in Egypt
1946/47 CE	Discovery of the Dead Sea Scrolls in the West Bank

APPENDIX B: THE CANONS COMPARED

	JUDAISM	BETA ISRAEL	WESTERN TRADITION	
	(Hebrew Bible)		Protestant	Roman Catholic
PENTATEUCH (TORAH)				
PROPHETS (NEVI'IM)				
WRITINGS (KETUVIM)				
TOBIT				
JUDITH				
BARUCH				
SIRACH				
1-2 MACCABEES				
WISDOM OF SOLOMON				
ADDITIONS TO ESTHER				
ADDITIONS TO DANIEL				
PSALM 151				
PRAYER OF MANASSEH				
JUBILEES				
1 ENOCH				
3 MACCABEES				
4 MACCABEES				
JOSIPPON				
1-3 MEQABYAN				
4 BARUCH				
2 ESDRAS		3-14 (4 Ezra)		
GOSPELS				
ACTS				
PAULINE EPISTLES				
CATHOLIC EPISTLES				
REVELATION				

Works included in biblical canons accepted by specific Jewish and Christian communities.

Works excluded from biblical canons accepted by specific Jewish and Christian communities.

| EASTERN ORTHODOX | ORIENTAL ORTHODOX | | ASSYRIAN CHURCH OF THE EAST |
	Armenian, Syriac, Coptic	Ethiopian Tewahedo	
	Armenian, Syriac		
Georgian			
		3–14 (4 Ezra)	

APPENDIX C: IMPORTANT FIGURES IN THE MODERN STUDY OF APOCRYPHA

JOHANN ALBERT FABRICIUS (1668–1736)

Published two of the earliest and most important modern anthologies of apocrypha: *Codex apocryphus Novi Testamenti* (1703) and *Codex pseudepigraphus Veteris Testamenti* (1713).

HEINRICH SIKE (1669–1712)

Published on biblical and apocryphal works, most notably the *Arabic Infancy Gospel: Evangelium infantiae, vel liber apocryphus de infantia servatoris* (1697).

JOHANN KARL THILO (1794–1853)

Published editions of apocrypha:

- *Codex Apocryphus Novi Testamenti* (1832)
- *Acts of Thomas* (1823)
- *Acts of Peter and Paul* (1838)
- *Acta Andreae et Matthiae apud Anthropophagos* (1846)
- *Acts of John* (1847)

CONSTANTIN VON TISCHENDORF (1815–1874)

Discovered the Codex Sinaiticus, the world's oldest and most complete Bible (ca. 330–60). Published anthologies of editions of apocrypha:

- *Acta Apostolorum apocrypha* (1851)
- *Evangelia apocrypha* (1853; 2nd edition 1876)
- *Apocalypses apocryphae* (1866)

WILLIAM WRIGHT (1830–1889)

Published about apocrypha, most notably *Contributions to the Apocryphal Literature of the New Testament* (1865).

AGNES SMITH LEWIS (1843–1926) AND
MARGARET DUNLOP GIBSON (1843–1920)

Discovered the Syriac Sinaiticus, an early Syriac translation of the Gospels (ca. 350–400). Published anthologies of editions and translations of apocrypha:

- Gibson, *Apocrypha Sinaitica* (1896)
- Gibson, *Apocrypha Arabica* (1901)
- Lewis, *Apocrypha Syriaca: The Protevangelium Jacobi and Transitus Mariae* (1902)
- Lewis, *Acta Mythologica Apostolorum* (1904)

R. H. CHARLES (1855–1931)

Published numerous editions, translations, and anthologies of apocrypha, most notably:

- *The Apocrypha and Pseudepigrapha of the Old Testament* (1913)
- Editions of *Jubilees, 1 Enoch, Baruch, Assumption of Moses, Ascension of Isaiah*
- *Testaments of the Twelve Patriarchs*

MONTAGUE RHODES JAMES (1862–1936)

Published anthologies of editions and translations of apocrypha:

- *Apocrypha Anecdota* (1893–1897)
- *The Lost Apocrypha of the Old Testament* (1920)
- *The Apocryphal New Testament* (1924)

LOUIS GINZBERG (1873–1953)

Published an anthology of early Jewish narratives, many from apocrypha, titled *The Legends of the Jews* (1909–1938).

FURTHER READING

In this book, I have introduced biblical apocrypha and highlighted a variety of representative works. But this book is only a beginning. This section contains useful resources—some of which were used in the research of this book—to further explore the world of apocrypha.

ONLINE SOURCES TO READ ORIGINAL APOCRYPHA

There are many websites where you can read translations of apocrypha, and I especially recommend:

Christian Classics Ethereal Library: CCEL.org

Early Christian Writings: EarlyChristianWritings.com

Early Jewish Writings: EarlyJewishWritings.com

The Gnostic Archive: Gnosis.org

Internet Sacred Text Archive: Sacred-Texts.com

You will find many other resources, including summaries and links to translations, on:

e-Clavis: Christian Apocrypha: NASSCAL.com/e-clavis-christian -apocrypha

BOOKS ON GNOSTICISM

For introductions to Gnosticism and the Nag Hammadi Codices, I suggest the following.

DeConick, April D. *The Gnostic New Age: How a Countercultural Spirituality Revolutionized Religion from Antiquity to Today.* New York: Columbia University Press, 2016.

Lewis, Nicola Denzey. *Introduction to "Gnosticism": Ancient Voices, Christian Worlds*. Oxford, UK: Oxford University Press, 2013.

Pagels, Elaine. *The Gnostic Gospels*. New York: Vintage Books, 1989.

SOURCES ON SECOND TEMPLE JUDAISM

Research on many early Jewish works and the Dead Sea Scrolls discussed in this book was sourced from the following:

Collins, John J. *The Dead Sea Scrolls: A Biography*. Princeton, NJ: Princeton University Press, 2012.

Docherty, Susan. *The Jewish Pseudepigrapha: An Introduction to the Literature of the Second Temple Period*. Minneapolis, MN: Fortress Press, 2015.

Gurtner, Daniel M. *Introducing the Pseudepigrapha of Second Temple Judaism: Message, Context, and Significance*. Grand Rapids, MI: Baker Academic, 2020.

Mroczek, Eva. *The Literary Imagination in Jewish Antiquity*. Oxford, UK: Oxford University Press, 2016.

Nickelsburg, George W. E. *Jewish Literature between the Bible and the Mishnah*, 2nd edition. Minneapolis, MN: Fortress Press, 2005.

VanderKam, James. "The Dead Sea Scrolls," in *Early Judaism: New Insights and Scholarship*, edited by Frederick E. Greenspahn. New York: New York University Press, 2018, pages 11–28. (Many of the other essays in this book are worth reading, especially those in the section titled "Early Diversity.")

DEUTEROCANONICAL WORKS

Many versions of the Bible include the deuterocanonical works, but I especially recommend the following:

Coogan, Michael D., editor. *The New Oxford Annotated Bible with the Apocrypha: New Revised Standard Version*, 4th edition. Oxford, UK: Oxford University Press, 2010.

Klawans, Jonathan, and Lawrence M. Wills, editors. *The Jewish Annotated Apocrypha*. Oxford, UK: Oxford University Press, 2020.

Pietersma, Albert, and Benjamin G. Wright, editors. *A New English Translation of the Septuagint*. Oxford, UK: Oxford University Press, 2007. Online at CCAT.sas.upenn.edu/nets/edition.

If you want a deeper dive into the details of the deuterocanonical books, check out:

deSilva, David A. *Introducing the Apocrypha: Message, Context, and Significance*, 2nd edition. Grand Rapids, MI: Baker Academic, 2018.

SECOND TEMPLE JEWISH WORKS

Second Temple Jewish works in translation can be found in the following collections:

Abegg, Martin J. Jr., Peter Flint, and Eugene Ulrich. *The Dead Sea Scrolls Bible: The Oldest Known Bible Translated for the First Time into English*. New York: HarperOne, 1999.

Bauckham, Richard, James R. Davila, and Alexander Panayotov, editors. *Old Testament Pseudepigrapha: More Noncanonical Scriptures*. Grand Rapids, MI: Eerdmans, 2013.

Charlesworth, James H., editor. *The Old Testament Pseudepigrapha*, 2 volumes. Garden City, NY: Doubleday, 1985.

Ginzberg, Louis. *Legends of the Jews*, translated by Henrietta Szold and Paul Radin, 2nd edition, 2 volumes. Philadelphia: Jewish Publication Society, 2003. (This includes retellings of many extra-biblical narratives from the periods of the Second Temple and Rabbinic Judaism.)

Vermes, Geza. *The Complete Dead Sea Scrolls in English*. New York: Allen Lane, 1997.

ORTHODOX TEWAHEDO WORKS

The following article is a good resource for the Orthodox Tewahedo Christian biblical canon:

Abraha, Tedros. "The Biblical Canon of the Orthodoks Täwahədo Church of Ethiopia and Eritrea," in *Il canone biblico nelle chiese orientali: atti del simposio, Pontificio Istituto orientale, Roma 23 marzo 2010*, edited by Edward G. Farrugia and Emidio Vergani. Rome: Pontificio Istituto orientale, 2017. Pages 95–122.

BOOKS ON CHRISTIAN APOCRYPHA

These books are useful for further general reading about apocrypha:

Bockmuehl, Markus. *Ancient Apocryphal Gospels*. Louisville, KY: Westminster John Knox Press, 2017.

Burke, Tony. *Secret Scriptures Revealed: A New Introduction to the Christian Apocrypha*. Grand Rapids, MI: Eerdmans, 2013.

de Bruin, Tom. *Extreme Walking: Extrabiblical Books and the Bible*. Eugene, OR: Cascade Books, 2018. (On reading apocrypha along with the Bible from a Christian perspective.)

Ehrman, Bart D. *Lost Scriptures: Books That Did Not Make It into the New Testament*. Oxford, UK: Oxford University Press, 2003.

Foster, Paul. *The Apocryphal Gospels: A Very Short Introduction*. Oxford, UK: Oxford University Press, 2009.

Jacobovici, Simcha, and Barrie Wilson. *The Lost Gospel: Decoding the Ancient Text That Reveals Jesus' Marriage to Mary the Magdalene*. New York: Pegasus, 2014.

Jenkins, Philip. *The Many Faces of Christ: The Thousand-Year Story of the Survival and Influence of the Lost Gospels*. New York: Basic Books, 2015.

Klauck, Hans-Josef. *The Apocryphal Acts of the Apostles: An Introduction*, translated by Brian McNeil. Waco, TX: Baylor University Press, 2008.

———. *Apocryphal Gospels: An Introduction*, translated by Brian McNeil. London: T&T Clark, 2003.

COLLECTIONS OF CHRISTIAN APOCRYPHA

The following books are good sources of translated Christian apocrypha:

Burke, Tony, editor. *New Testament Apocrypha: More Noncanonical Scriptures, Volume 2*. Grand Rapids, MI: Eerdmans, 2020.

Burke, Tony, and Brent Landau, editors. *New Testament Apocrypha: More Noncanonical Scriptures, Volume 1*. Grand Rapids, MI: Eerdmans, 2016.

Ehrman, Bart D., and Zlatko Pleše. *The Apocryphal Gospels: Texts and Translations*. Oxford, UK: Oxford University Press, 2011.

Elliott, J. K. *The Apocryphal New Testament: A Collection of Apocryphal Christian Literature in an English Translation*. Oxford, UK: Oxford University Press, 1993.

Hennecke, Edgar, and Wilhelm Schneemelcher, editors. *New Testament Apocrypha*, translated by R. McL. Wilson, revised edition, 2 volumes. Louisville, KY: Westminster John Knox Press, 1992.

Meyer, Marvin, editor. *The Nag Hammadi Scriptures: The International Edition*. New York: HarperOne, 2007.

BOOKS ON REVELATIONS AND APOCALYPSES

On the genre of apocalyptic literature, the following are key introductions:

Collins, John J. *The Apocalyptic Imagination: An Introduction to Jewish Apocalyptic Literature*, 2nd edition. Grand Rapids, MI: Eerdmans, 1998.

Himmelfarb, Martha. *The Apocalypse: A Brief History*. Malden, MA: Wiley-Blackwell, 2010.

Pagels, Elaine. *Revelations: Visions, Prophecy, and Politics in the Book of Revelation*. New York: Penguin, 2012.

Portier-Young, Anathea E. *Apocalypse against Empire: Theologies of Resistance in Early Judaism*. Grand Rapids, MI: Eerdmans, 2011.

THE EARLY JEWISH AND CHRISTIAN BIBLICAL CANON

For a collection of early Jewish and Christian lists of the biblical canon with translations, see the following:

Gallagher, Edmon L., and John D. Meade. *The Biblical Canon Lists from Early Christianity: Texts and Analysis*. Oxford, UK: Oxford University Press, 2017.

HOW APOCRYPHA WAS DEFINED AND CATEGORIZED

The following articles discuss modern construction of definitions and categories such as "apocrypha," "pseudepigrapha," "orthodoxy," "heresy," and "diversity."

DiTommaso, Lorenzo. "The 'Old Testament Pseudepigrapha' as Category and Corpus," in *A Guide to Early Jewish Texts and Traditions in Christian Transmission*, edited by Alexander Kulik, David Hamidović, Gabriele Boccaccini, Lorenzo DiTommaso, and Michael E. Stone. Oxford, UK: Oxford University Press, 2019. Pages 258–80.

King, Karen L. "Factions, Variety, Diversity, Multiplicity: Representing Early Christian Differences for the 21st Century," *Method & Theory in the Study of Religion* 23 (2011): 216–37.

Reed, Annette Yoshiko. "The Afterlives of New Testament Apocrypha," *Journal of Biblical Literature* 134 (2015): 401–25.

———. "The Modern Invention of 'Old Testament Pseudepigrapha,'" *Journal of Theological Studies* 60 (2009): 403–36.

INDEX

Essenes, 51–53

Esther, additions to, 28–29

Ezra. See *2 Esdras*

F

Fabricius, Johann Albert, 65,
    70, 98, 100, 117, 121

*Fifteen Signs Before
    Judgment Day*, 126

Flint, Peter, 51

G

Ge'ez, 11

Genesis apocryphon, 63

Gnostic texts
    about, 79–80
    Apocalypse of Adam, 93
    Gospel of Judas, 90–92
    Gospel of Mary, 88–90
    Gospel of Philip, 86–88
    Gospel of Truth, 81–83
    *Prayer of the Apostle
        Paul*, 92–93
    Secret Book of John, 83–85
    Thunder: Perfect Mind, 93

Gospel of Judas, 90–92

Gospel of Mary, 12, 88–90

Gospel of Nicodemus, 13, 76–78

Gospel of Philip, 86–88

Gospel of Pseudo-Matthew, 13,
    67–69, 71

Gospel of Thomas, 14, 73–76, 101

Gospel of Truth, 81–83

Gospels, 64

Grabe, John Ernest, 98

Great Psalms Scroll, 57–59

Grébault, Sylvain, 105, 119

Greek, 11

Gregory the Great, Pope, 110

Grenfell, Bernard Pyne, 74

Guerrier, Louis, 105

H

Hagiography, 95

Hauler, Edmund, 124

Hebrew Bible
    about, 2–4, 33–34
    Alphabet of Ben Sira, 44–45
    4 Baruch, 49
    Book of Jasher, 46–47
    Joseph and Aseneth, 38–40
    Josippon, 48
    Jubilees, 36–38
    Life of Adam and Eve, 34–36
    3 Maccabees, 40–42
    4 Maccabees, 42–43
    1–3 Meqabyan, 48–49

Hebrew language, 11

Hunt, Arthur Surridge, 74, 88

Hymn of the Bride, 101

Hymn of the Pearl, 101, 102

I

Infancy Gospel of James, 65–67

Infancy Gospel of Thomas,
    69–71, 106

J

Jacobovici, Simcha, 39

Jagic, Victor, 34

Jerome, 5, 72, 110

Jesus
    Gospel of Judas, 90–92
    Gospel of Mary, 88–90

ACKNOWLEDGMENTS

Writing this book has been a pleasure—especially revisiting apocrypha I haven't encountered in years and finding new ways to think about some of my favorites. I'm indebted to a number of people who helped along the way. I'm happy to thank the team at Callisto, especially Joe Cho, Lauren O'Neal, Adrian Potts, and Virginia Bhashkar. To Judy, Catie, and Maggie: thank you for patience while I wrote this book in pandemic lockdown. For encouragement, help with research, discussions about apocrypha, and feedback, I owe thanks to Tony Burke, Tom de Bruin, Tim Hawk, Stephen Hopkins, Amity Reading, Janet Spittler, and Charlie Wright. I'm appreciative for years of conversation with members of the North American Society for the Study of Christian Apocryphal Literature (NASSCAL), who continually remind me why I love apocrypha studies.

Finally, now that the book is out of my hands, I'm grateful to all of you who will read it. As the dedication says, this book is for my students: those I teach in the classroom and anyone who learns from my work. Thank you for reading.

ABOUT THE AUTHOR

BRANDON W. HAWK is an associate professor of English at Rhode Island College, with expertise in medieval literature and the transmission of the Bible and apocrypha. He has published two books: *Preaching Apocrypha in Anglo-Saxon England* (2018) and *The Gospel of Pseudo-Matthew and the Nativity of Mary* (2019). You can find him at BrandonWHawk.net and on Twitter @b_hawk.

CPSIA information can be obtained
at www.ICGtesting.com
Printed in the USA
JSHW040259210821
17936JS00002B/2